1, 2 Thessalonians

THE CROSSWAY CLASSIC COMMENTARIES

1, 2 Thessalonians

by

John Calvin

Series Editors

Alister McGrath and J. I. Packer

CROSSWAY BOOKS

A DIVISION OF GOOD NEWS PUBLISHERS

WHEATON, ILLINOIS • NOTTINGHAM, ENGLAND

1, 2 Thessalonians

Copyright © 1999 by Watermark

Published by Crossway Books
      A division of Good News Publishers
      1300 Crescent Street
      Wheaton, Illinois 60187

First printing, 1999

Printed in the United States of America

Library of Congress Cataloging-in-Publication Data
Calvin, John, 1509-1564.
    1, 2 Thessalonians / by John Calvin.
      p.   cm. — (The Crossway classic commentaries)
    ISBN 1-58134-117-2 (pbk. : alk. paper)
    1. Bible. N.T. Thessalonians—Commentaries Early works to 1800.
I. Title. II. Title: First, second Thessalonians. III. Series.
BS2725.3.C35 1999   99-29562
227'.81077—dc21   CIP

| 15 | 14 | 13 | 12 | 11 | 10 | 09 | 08 | 07 | 06 | 05 | 04 | 03 | 02 | 01 | 00 | 99 |
| 15 | 14 | 13 | 12 | 11 | 10 | 9 | 8 | 7 | 6 | 5 | 4 | 3 | 2 | 1 |

First British edition 1999

Production and Printing in the United States of America for
CROSSWAY BOOKS
Norton Street, Nottingham, England NG7 3HR

ISBN 1-85684-193-6

Contents

Series Preface

The purpose of the Crossway Classic Commentaries is to make some of the most valuable commentaries on the books of the Bible, by some of the greatest Bible teachers and theologians in the last 500 years, available to a new generation. These books will help today's readers learn truth, wisdom, and devotion from such authors as J. C. Ryle, Martin Luther, John Calvin, J. B. Lightfoot, John Owen, Charles Spurgeon, Charles Hodge, and Matthew Henry.

We do not apologize for the age of some of the items chosen. In the realm of practical exposition promoting godliness, the old is often better than the new. Spiritual vision and authority, based on an accurate handling of the biblical text, are the qualities that have been primarily sought in deciding what to include.

So far as is possible, everything is tailored to the needs and enrichment of thoughtful readers—lay Christians, students, and those in the ministry. The originals, some of which were written at a high technical level, have been abridged as needed, simplified stylistically, and unburdened of foreign words. However, the intention of this series is never to change any thoughts of the original authors, but to faithfully convey them in an understandable fashion.

The publishers are grateful to Dr. Alister McGrath of Wycliffe Hall, Oxford, Dr. J. I. Packer of Regent College, Vancouver, and Watermark of Norfolk, England, for the work of selecting and editing that now brings this project to fruition.

THE PUBLISHERS
Crossway Books
Wheaton, Illinois

Introduction

John Calvin fashioned the *Institutes*, from the second edition on, as a lead-in not only to the biblical faith as such, but also to the commentaries he planned to write. Having thus put all his analytical, historical, pastoral, and polemical discussions of doctrines into a separate book, he felt free in the commentaries to follow undistractedly a running style of textual exposition that would bring out in an applicatory way the two-in-one reality of what was there—namely, the mind of God the Holy Spirit expressed in and communicated through the words in which the human writer expressed his own mind. A divine work no less miraculous than the Incarnation itself had produced an identity of the writer's message with the instruction of God, and the commentator's business was to elucidate this by means of what we might call both-and exposition—exposition, that is, that moved through didactic declarations of the writer, witnessing to God, to the *doctrina* (teaching) of God himself in and through these declarations in their canonical context.

So Calvin's work as a biblical interpreter was always shaped and controlled by three linked thoughts: first, this is what the writer had to say about God to his own envisaged readership; second, this is what the Holy Spirit of God had to say to those same people; third, this is what the Holy Spirit of God had to say to all who read the words thereafter, ourselves included. By consistently following this approach, with linguistic skill, good literary judgment, and theological and spiritual insight unmatched in the sixteenth century (and hardly ever equaled since), Calvin produced commentaries that are deservedly designated as classics. Several have already appeared in this series, and here is another.

The letters to the Thessalonians are often treated as minor items in Calvin's output, but this is wrong. Granted, they are not massive doctrinal treatises like those on Romans and Galatians and Ephesians and Colossians; nor do they get expansive on relational matters as, in their different ways, do the Corinthian letters and Philippians; nor are they heavy pep talks in the manner of the Pastorals, where Paul admonished his juniors, now his deputies, with the intense, breathy seriousness that we associate with Jewish parents still. The Thessalonian letters are by comparison cheerful and brisk, but they are not in any sense lightweight. They are forthright pastoral missives spelling out in blunt, on-the-nose terms aspects of faith, love, hope, and holiness that some of the new Thessalonian believers, the spiritual fruit of Paul's three-week ministry there, either had not yet grasped or were already in danger of forgetting.

Calvin draws us into the same world of discipleship in which these Thessalonians had come to live and gently but firmly presses on us as he goes along the moral and spiritual challenges that Paul was presenting to his converts. First published in 1551, with 1 Thessalonians dedicated to Calvin's former Latin teacher and 2 Thessalonians to his family doctor, these expositions impact one's spiritual system like a course of vitamin tablets; they leave you stronger and more energetic. Try them and see.

J. I. PACKER

1 Thessalonians

Dedication

The author's dedicatory letter to Maturinus Corderius, a man of eminent piety and learning, principal of the College of Lausanne.

It is befitting that you should come in for a share in my labors, inasmuch as, under your auspices, having entered on a course of study, I made proficiency at least so far as to be prepared to profit in some degree the church of God. When my father sent me, while yet a boy, to Paris, after I had simply tasted the first elements of the Latin tongue, Providence so ordered it that I had, for a short time, the privilege of having you as my instructor, that I might be taught by you the true method of learning, in such a way that I might be prepared afterwards to make somewhat better proficiency. For, after presiding over the first class with the highest renown, on observing that pupils who had been ambitiously trained up by the other masters produced nothing but mere show, nothing of solidity, so that they required to be formed by you anew, tired of this annoyance, you that year descended to the fourth class. This, indeed, was what you had in view, but to me it was a singular kindness on the part of God that I happened to have an auspicious commencement of such a course of training. And although I was permitted to have the use of it only for a short time, from the circumstance that we were soon afterward advanced higher by an injudicious man, who regulated our studies according to his own pleasure, or rather his caprice, yet I derived so much assistance afterward from your training that it is with good reason that I acknowledge myself indebted to you for such progress as has since been made. And this I was desirous to testify to posterity, that, if any advantage shall accrue to them from my writings, they shall know that it has in some degree originated with you.

John Calvin, Geneva, 17 February, 1550

Argument of the First Letter to the Thessalonians

The greater part of this letter consists of exhortations. Paul had instructed the Thessalonians in the right faith. On hearing, however, that persecutions were raging there, he had sent Timothy with the view of preparing them for the conflict, that they might not give way through fear, as human infirmity is apt to do. Having been afterwards informed by Timothy about their entire condition, he employs various arguments to confirm them in steadfastness of faith, as well as in endurance, should they be called to endure anything for the testimony of the Gospel. These things he treats in the first three chapters.

At the beginning of chapter 4, he exhorts them, in general terms, to holiness of life; afterwards he recommends mutual benevolence and all offices that flow from it. Toward the end, however, he touches upon the question of the resurrection and explains in what way we shall all be raised up from death. From this it is clear that there were some wicked or light-minded people who endeavored to unsettle their faith by unseasonably bringing forward many frivolous things. Hence with the view of cutting off all pretext for foolish and needless disputings, he instructs them in few words as to the views that they should entertain.

In the fifth chapter he prohibits them, even more strictly, from inquiring about the timing of our Lord's return. He admonishes them to be always on the watch, in case they should be taken by surprise by Christ's sudden and unexpected approach. From this he proceeds to employ various exhortations and then concludes the letter.

1 Thessalonians
Chapter 1

Verse 1

Paul, Silas and Timothy, To the church of the Thessalonians in God the Father and the Lord Jesus Christ: Grace and peace to you.

1. The brevity of the inscription clearly shows that Paul's teaching had been received with reverence among the Thessalonians, and that without controversy they all rendered to him the honor that he deserved. For when in other letters he designated himself an apostle, he did so for the purpose of claiming for himself authority. Hence the circumstance here, simply making use of his own name without any title of honor, is proof that those to whom he writes voluntarily acknowledged him to be such as he was. The ministers of Satan, it is true, had endeavored to trouble this church also, but it is evident that their machinations were fruitless.

He also associates others along with himself, in common with himself, as the authors of the letter. Nothing further is stated here that has not been explained elsewhere, except that he says, **the church . . . in God the Father and . . . Christ,** by which terms he intimates that there is truly among the Thessalonians a church of God. This mark, therefore, is as it were an approval of a true and lawful church. We may, however, at the same time infer from it that a church is to be sought only where God presides and where Christ reigns, and that, in short, there is no church but that which is founded upon God, is gathered under the auspices of Christ, and is united in his name.

Verses 2-5

We always thank God for all of you, mentioning you in our prayers. We continually remember before our God and Father your work produced by faith, your labor prompted by love, and your endurance

inspired by hope in our Lord Jesus Christ. For we knew, brothers loved by God, that he has chosen you, because our gospel came to you not simply with words, but also with power, with the Holy Spirit and with deep conviction. You know how we lived among you for your sake.

2. We always thank God for all of you. He praises, as he is wont, their faith and other virtues, not so much, however, for the purpose of praising them as to exhort them to perseverance. For it is no small spur to eagerness of pursuit when we reflect that God has adorned us with special endowments, that he may finish what he has begun, and that we have, under his guidance and direction, advanced in the right course in order that we may reach the goal. Just as a vain confidence in those virtues that men foolishly arrogate to themselves puffs them up with pride and makes them careless and indolent for the time to come, so a recognition of the gifts of God humbles pious minds and stirs them up to anxious concern. Hence, instead of congratulations, the apostle makes use of thanksgiving, that he may put them in mind that everything in them that he declares to be worthy of praise is a kindness of God. He also turns immediately to the future in making mention of his **prayers**.

3. We continually remember. While the adverb **continually** might be taken in connection with what goes before, it suits better to connect it in this manner. What follows might also be rendered "remembering your work of faith and labor of love."

Paul assigns a reason, however, why he cherishes so strong an affection toward them and prays diligently on their behalf—because he perceived in them those gifts of God that should stir him up to cherish love and respect toward them. And unquestionably, the more anyone excels in piety and other excellencies, so much more ought we to hold him in regard and esteem. For what or who is more worthy of love than God? Hence there is nothing that should tend more to excite our love to individuals than when the Lord manifests himself in them by the gifts of his Spirit. This is the highest commendation of all among the pious, the most sacred bond of connection by which they are more especially bound to each other.

Your work produced by faith. I understand this as meaning the effect of it. This effect, however, may be explained in two ways—passively or actively, either as meaning that faith was in itself a special token of the power and efficacy of the Holy Spirit, inasmuch as he has wrought powerfully in the exciting of it, or as meaning that it afterwards produced its fruits outwardly. I reckon the effect to be in the root of faith rather than in its fruits—"a rare energy of faith has shown itself powerfully in you."

He adds, **your labor prompted by love,** by which he means that in the cultivation of love they had not scorned trouble or labor. Assuredly, it is known through experience how hard-working love is. That age, however, more especially afforded to believers a manifold sphere of labor if they desired to discharge the offices of love. The church was dreadfully pressed down by a great number of afflictions. Many were stripped of their wealth, many were fugitives from their country, many were destitute of counsel, many were tender and weak. The condition of almost all was involved. So many cases of distress did not allow **love** to be inactive.

To **hope** he assigns **endurance**, as it is always linked with it (see Romans 8:25). So the statement should be explained as meaning that Paul remembers their endurance in hoping for the coming of Christ. From this we may gather a brief definition of true Christianity—it is a faith that is living and full of vigor, so that it spares no labor when assistance is to be given to one's neighbors. On the contrary, all the pious employ themselves diligently in offices of love and lay out their efforts so that, intent upon the hope of the manifestation of Christ, they despise everything else and, armed with endurance, rise above the wearisomeness of length of time as well as above all the temptations of the world.

The clause **before our God and Father** may be viewed as referring to Paul's remembrance or to the three things spoken about immediately before. I explain it in this way: As he had spoken of his **prayers**, he declares that as often as he raises his thoughts to the kingdom of God, he at the same time recalls to his remembrance the **faith**, **hope**, and **endurance** of the Thessalonians. As all mere pretense must vanish when people come into the presence of God, this is added in order that the affirmation may have more weight. Further, by this declaration of his goodwill toward them he designed to make them more teachable and prepared to listen.

4. The word **know** may apply to Paul as well as to the Thessalonians. Erasmus refers it to the Thessalonians. I prefer to follow Chrysostom, who understands it of Paul and of his colleagues, for it is, it appears to me, a more ample confirmation of the previous statement. God himself had testified by many tokens that they were acceptable and dear to him.

He has chosen you. I am not altogether dissatisfied with the interpretation given by Chrysostom—that God had made the Thessalonians illustrious and had established their excellence. Paul, however, had it in view to express something further, for he touches on their calling; as there had appeared in that calling no common marks of God's power, he infers from this that they had been especially called with evidences of a sure election. For the reason is immediately added that it was a bare preaching that had been brought to them, but such as was linked with the efficacy of the Holy Spirit, that it might obtain entire credit among them.

5. When he says, **with power, with the Holy Spirit**, it is, in my opinion, as if he had said, "in the power *of* the Holy Spirit," so that the latter term is added to explain the former term. **With deep conviction** was either in the thing itself or in the disposition of the Thessalonians. I am rather

inclined to think that the meaning is, Paul's gospel had been confirmed by solid proofs, as though God had shown from heaven that he had ratified their calling. When, however, Paul brings forward the proofs by which he had felt assured that the calling of the Thessalonians was altogether from God, he takes occasion at the same time to recommend his ministry, that they may themselves also recognize him and his colleagues as having been raised up by God.

By the term **power** some understand miracles. I extend it further, as referring to the spiritual energy of right doctrine. God's calling, which is in itself hidden, is manifested when he gathers to himself the lost sheep and joins them to his flock and holds out his hand to those who were wandering and estranged from him. Hence a knowledge of our election must be sought from this source. As, however, the secret counsel of God is a labyrinth to those who disregard his calling, so those act perversely who, under the pretext of faith and calling, darken this first grace, from which faith itself flows. "By faith," they say, "we obtain salvation. There is therefore no eternal predestination of God that distinguishes between us and reprobates." It is as though they said, "Salvation is from faith; there is, therefore, no grace of God that illuminates us in faith." But it is not so. Rather, as gratuitous election must be linked with calling and with its effect, so it must necessarily hold the first place.

Paul's aim is that the Thessalonians, influenced by the same considerations, may entertain no doubt that they were chosen by God. For it had been God's design, in honoring Paul's ministry, that he might manifest to them their adoption. Accordingly, having said that they **know how we lived among you,** he immediately adds that he was what he was **for your sake,** by which he means that all this had been given them in order that they might be fully persuaded that they were loved by God and that their election was beyond all question.

Verses 6-8

You became imitators of us and of the Lord; in spite of severe suffering, you welcomed the message with the joy given by the Holy Spirit. And so you became a model to all the believers in Macedonia and Achaia. The Lord's message rang out from you not only in Macedonia and Achaia—your faith in God has become known everywhere. Therefore we do not need to say anything about it.

6. With the view of increasing their alacrity, he declares that there is a mutual agreement and harmony as it were between his preaching and their faith. Unless men, for their part, answer to God, no proficiency will follow from the grace that is offered to them. It is not as though they could do this of themselves, but God, as he begins our salvation by calling us, completes it by fashioning our hearts to obedience. The sum, therefore, is that an evidence of divine election showed itself not only in Paul's ministry, insofar as it was furnished with the power of the Holy Spirit, but also in the faith of the Thessalonians, so that this conformity is a powerful attestation of it. He says, however, **You became imitators of us and of the Lord,** in the same sense in which it is said that the people believed God and his servant Moses (see Exodus 4:30-31)—not that Paul and Moses had anything different than God, but because he wrought powerfully by them, as his ministers and instruments. **You welcomed.** Their readiness in receiving the Gospel is called an imitation of God for this reason: God had presented himself to the Thessalonians, and they had voluntarily come forward to meet him.

He says **with the joy given by the Holy Spirit** so we may know it is not by the instigation of the flesh or the promptings of their own nature that men will be ready and eager to obey God; this is the work of God's Spirit. The circumstance—**in spite of severe suffering** they had embraced the Gospel—gives us greater understanding. We see many, not otherwise disinclined to the Gospel, who nevertheless avoid it because they are intimidated by a fear of the cross. Those, accordingly, who do not hesitate to embrace along with the Gospel the afflictions that threaten them furnish an admirable example of magnanimity. And from this it is so clearly apparent how necessary it is that the Spirit should aid us in this, for the Gospel cannot be properly or sincerely received unless it be with a joyful heart. Nothing, however, is more at variance with our natural disposition than to rejoice in afflictions.

7. Here we have another amplification—they had even stirred up believers by their example. It is a great thing to be so decidedly impacted by the start of those who had entered upon the course before us as to furnish assistance to them as they follow that course.

A model. *Typos* (the word Paul uses) is employed by the Greeks in the same sense as *exemplar* is among Latin speakers and *parton* among the French. He says, then, that the courage of the Thessalonians had been so illustrious that other believers had borrowed from them a rule of constancy. I prefer, however, to render it *pattern*, that I might not needlessly make any change upon the Greek phrase made use of by Paul. Furthermore, the plural number expresses, in my opinion, something more than if he had said that that church as a body had been set forward for imitation; there were as many *patterns* as there were individuals.

8. **The Lord's message rang out from you.** Here we have an elegant metaphor by which he intimates that their faith was so alive that it **rang out,** as it were, arousing other nations. The Word of God **rang out** from them inasmuch as their faith resounded loud and clear, bringing credit to the Gospel. He says this had not only occurred in neighboring places, but

this **message** had extended far and wide and had been distinctly heard, so that the matter did not need to be published and extolled by him.

Verses 9-10

For they themselves report what kind of reception you gave us. They tell how you turned to God from idols to serve the living and true God, and to wait for his Son from heaven, whom he raised from the dead— Jesus, who rescues us from the coming wrath.

He says that the report of their conversion had obtained great renown everywhere. When he mentions **what kind of reception** they gave him, he refers to the power of the Spirit, by which God had adorned and magnificently attested his Gospel. He says, however, that both things are freely reported among other nations as things worthy of mention. In the detail that follows, he shows, first, what the condition of mankind is before the Lord enlightens them by the teaching of his Gospel, and further, for what end he would have us instructed, and what is the fruit of the Gospel. For although not all worship idols, all are nevertheless addicted to idolatry and are immersed in blindness and madness. Hence, it is owing to the kindness of God that we are exempted from the pretenses of the devil and every kind of superstition. Some, indeed, God converts earlier, others later; but as alienation is common to all, it is necessary that we be converted to God before we can serve him. From this also we gather the essence and nature of true faith, inasmuch as no one gives due credit to God but the man who, renouncing the vanity of his own understanding, embraces and receives the pure worship of God.

9. To serve the living and true God. This is the purpose and effect of genuine conversion. We see, indeed, that many leave off superstitions who nevertheless after taking this step are so far from making progress in piety that they fall into what is worse. Having thrown off all regard for God, they give themselves up to a profane and brutal contempt of all religion. Thus, in ancient times the superstitions of the vulgar were derided by Epicurus, Diogenes the Cynic, and the like, but in such a way that they mixed up the worship of God so as to make no difference between it and absurd trifles. Hence we must take care lest the pulling down of errors is followed by the overthrow of faith. Further, the apostle, in ascribing to God the epithets **true** and **living**, indirectly censures idols as being dead and worthless inventions and as being falsely called gods. He makes the end of conversion to be what I have noted—that they might **serve the living and true God**. Hence the teaching of the Gospel induces us to serve and obey God. For so long as we are the servants of sin, we are free from righteousness (see Romans 6:20), inasmuch as we delude ourselves and wander here and there, exempt from any yoke. No one, therefore, is properly converted to God but the man who has learned to place himself wholly under subjection to God.

10. As, however, this matter is extremely difficult, appealing to the great corruption of our nature, the apostle shows us at the same time what it is that retains and confirms us in the fear of God and obedience to him — **to wait for his Son.** For unless we are stirred up to the hope of eternal life, the world will quickly draw us to itself. As it is only confidence in the divine goodness that induces us to serve God, so it is only the expectation of final redemption that keeps us from giving way and losing heart. Let every one, therefore, who wants to persevere in the path of a holy life apply his whole mind to an expectation of Christ's coming. It is also worthy of notice that Paul uses the expression **to wait for his Son** instead of the hope of everlasting salvation. For, unquestionably, without Christ we are ruined and thrown into despair; but when Christ shows himself, life and prosperity do at the same time shine forth upon us. Let us bear in mind, however, that this is said to believers exclusively, for he will come to be the Judge of the wicked, and they can do nothing but tremble in looking for him.

The apostle afterwards adds that **Jesus . . . rescues us from the coming wrath.** This is felt by none but those who, being reconciled to God by faith, have had their conscience already pacified; otherwise his name is dreadful. Christ, it is true, delivered us by his death from the anger of God; but the import of that deliverance will become apparent on the last day. This statement, however, consists of two sections. The first is that God's wrath and everlasting destruction are impending over the human race, inasmuch as everyone has sinned and fallen short of God's glory (see Romans 3:23). The second is, there is no way of escape but through Christ's grace, for it is not without good grounds that Paul assigns to him this office. It is, however, an inestimable gift that the pious, whenever mention is made of judgment, know that Christ will come as a Redeemer to them.

In addition to this Paul says emphatically, **the coming wrath,** that he may rouse up pious minds, lest they should fail from looking at the present life. Just as faith is looking at things that do not appear (see Hebrews 11:1), so nothing is less befitting than that we should estimate the wrath of God as however anyone is afflicted in this world; nothing is more absurd than to take hold of the transient blessings we enjoy and from them form an estimate of God's favor. While, therefore, on the one hand the wicked entertain themselves at their ease and we on the other hand languish in misery, let us learn to fear the vengeance of God, which is hidden from the eyes of flesh, and take our satisfaction in the secret delights of the spiritual life that we do not see.

Whom he raised from the dead. The apostle mentions here Christ's resurrection, on which the hope of our resurrection is founded, for death surrounds us everywhere. Hence, unless we learn to look to Christ, our minds will give way at every turn. By the same consideration, he admonishes them that Christ is to be waited for **from heaven**, because we will find nothing in the world to bear us up and make us remain firm, though there are innumerable trials to overwhelm us. Another circumstance must be noted: as Christ rose for this purpose—that he might make us all at length, as being his members, partakers of the same glory with himself—Paul intimates that Christ's resurrection would be in vain unless he again appeared as their Redeemer and extended to the whole body of the church the fruit and effect of that power that he once showed in his own person.

1 Thessalonians
Chapter 2

Verses 1-4

You know, brothers, that our visit to you was not a failure. We had previously suffered and been insulted in Philippi, as you know, but with the help of our God we dared to tell you his gospel in spite of strong opposition. For the appeal we make does not spring from error or impure motives, nor are we trying to trick you. On the contrary, we speak as men approved by God to be entrusted with the gospel. We are not trying to please men but God, who tests our hearts.

1-2. The apostle now, leaving out of view the testimony of other churches, reminds the Thessalonians of what they had themselves experienced and seen and explains at length in what way he, and his two associates as well, had conducted themselves among them. This was of the greatest importance for confirming the Thessalonians' faith. The reason Paul declares his integrity is so that the Thessalonians may perceive that they had been called to the faith not so much by a mortal man as by God himself. He says, therefore, that his **visit** to them **was not a failure** (v. 1). Ambitious people manifest much show, but they have nothing of substance. He uses the word **failure** here to imply a contrasting effectiveness.

He supports this with two arguments. The first is that he had suffered persecution and ignominy at Philippi; the second is that a great conflict was prepared at Thessalonica. We know that people's minds are weakened, indeed are altogether broken down, by shameful humiliation and persecutions. It was therefore evidence of a divine work that Paul, who had been subjected to evils of various kinds, behaved as if he was in a perfectly sound state, not hesitating to make an attempt on a large and opulent city, with the view of subjecting its inhabitants to Christ. In this **visit**, nothing is seen that savors of vain ostentation. In the second place the divine power is seen in that he did not discharge his duty with applause and favor but with conflict. Yet he stood firm and undaunted, from which it appears that he was sustained and strengthened by God's hand. This is what he means when he says that he **dared tell you his gospel in spite of strong opposition**. Unquestionably, if all these circumstances are carefully considered, it cannot be denied that God displayed his power magnificently there. The story is to be found in Acts 16—17.

3. For the appeal we make. He now uses another argument to confirm the Thessalonians in the faith they had embraced. Inasmuch as they had been faithfully and purely instructed in the Word of the Lord, he maintains that his teaching was free from all deception and uncleanness. And in order to place this matter beyond all doubt, he calls their conscience to witness. The three terms he uses may be distinguished, it would seem, in this way: **error** may refer to the substance of teaching, **impure motives** to the affections of the heart, and **trying to trick you** to a manner of acting. In the first place, therefore, he says they had not been deluded or imposed on by fallacies when they welcomed the kind of teaching he had given them. Second, he declares his integrity inasmuch as he had not come to them under the influence of any impure desire but acted solely by upright disposition. Third, he says he had done nothing fraudulently or maliciously but had on the contrary manifested a simplicity befitting a minister of Christ. As these things were well known to the Thessalonians, they had a sufficiently firm foundation for their faith.

4. We speak as men approved by God. The apostle now goes even higher, appealing to God as the Author of his apostleship. He reasons in this way: "God, when he assigned me this office, bore witness to me as a faithful servant; there is no reason, therefore, why men should have doubts as to my fidelity, which they know to have been **approved by God**." Paul, however, does not glory in having been **approved**, as though this came from himself; he is not here arguing about what he had by nature, nor is he opposing his own power to God's grace, but he simply says that the Gospel had been committed to him as a faithful and approved servant. God approves of those whom he has formed for himself according to his own pleasure.

We are not trying to please men. What is meant by pleasing men is seen in the contrast between pleasing *men* and pleasing *God*, for these things are opposed to each other. Further, when he says **God, who tests our hearts**, he is intimating that those who endeavor to obtain human favor are not influenced by an upright conscience and do nothing from the heart. Let us grasp, therefore, that true ministers of the Gospel ought to make it their aim to devote to God their endeavors, and to do this from the heart—not from any outward regard for the world, but because conscience tells them this is right and proper. Thus they will not make it their aim to **please men**; that is, they will not act under the influence of ambition, with a view to obtaining other people's favor.

Verses 5-8

You know we never used flattery, nor did we put on a mask to cover up greed—God is our witness. We were not looking for praise from men, not from you or anyone else. As apostles of Christ we could have been a burden to you, but we were gentle among you, like a mother caring for her little children. We loved you so much that we were delighted to share with you not only the gospel of God but our lives as well, because you had become so dear to us.

5. You know. It is not without good reason that the apostle so frequently repeats that the Thessalonians knew that what he states is true. There is no surer attestation than the experience of those with whom we speak. Paul mentions that he had conducted himself with integrity in order that his doctrine should be respected more, for the building up of their faith. This is also, however, a confirmation of the previous statement, for anyone who wants to please other people must of necessity stoop shamefully to flattery, while those who do their duty with an earnest and upright disposition will avoid all appearance of flattery.

When he adds, **nor did we put on a mask to cover up greed**, he means that when he was teaching among them he was not seeking his own personal gain. The apostle is saying, "I have not abused the Gospel, making it an occasion of gaining anything for myself." As, however, people's avarice and ambition frequently lie concealed, he calls God to witness. Here he mentions two vices (**flattery** and **greed**), from which he declares himself to be exempt and in so doing teaches that the servants of Christ should stand aloof from them. Thus, if we would distinguish the genuine servants of Christ from those who are hypocritical and spurious, they must be tried according to this rule; and everyone who wants to serve Christ correctly must conform to this same rule in aims and actions. Where avarice and ambition reign, innumerable corruptions follow, and the whole person succumbs to vanity, for these are the two sources from which the corruption of the whole ministry takes its rise.

7. We could have been a burden to you. Paul says he was so far removed from vain pomp, boasting, and arrogance that he even waived his just claim as far as the maintenance of authority was concerned. Inasmuch as he was an apostle of Christ, he deserved to be received with a higher degree of respect; but he had refrained from all appearance of preeminence, as though he was a minister of ordinary rank. From this it appears how far removed he was from all haughtiness and presumption.

We were gentle among you. The word **gentle** may be translated "mild," and there is no doubt that the apostle means voluntary abasement and humility.

Like a mother caring for her little children. "As if a nurse." In making this comparison he takes in two points he had touched on—that he had sought neither glory nor gain among the Thessalonians. A mother nursing her infant shows nothing of power or dignity. Paul says that he was such inasmuch as he voluntarily refrained from claiming the honor that was due to him and with calmness and modesty stooped to every kind of office. Second, a mother nursing her children manifests a certain rare and wonderful affection, inasmuch as she spares no labor and trouble, shuns no anxiety, is worn out by no labor, and even with cheerfulness of spirit gives herself to her child. In the same way Paul declares that he was so disposed toward the Thessalonians that he was prepared to lay out his life for their benefit. This, assuredly, was not the conduct of a man who was sordid or avaricious but of one who exercised an intimate affection, and he expresses this in the last part of the next verse (8): **because you had become so dear to us.** In the meantime, we must bear in mind that those who want to be ranked among true pastors must exercise this disposition of Paul—having more regard for the welfare of the church than for their own life, and not being impelled to seek their own advantage, but having a sincere love that they bear to those to whom they know God has tied and bound them.

Verses 9-12

Surely you remember, brothers, our toil and hardship; we worked night and day in order not to be a burden to anyone while we preached the gospel of God to you. You are witnesses, and so is God, of how holy, righteous and blameless we were among you who believed. For you know that we dealt with each of you as a father deals with his own children, encouraging, comforting and urging you to live lives worthy of God, who calls you into his kingdom and glory.

9. Surely you remember. These things tend to confirm what the apostle had stated previously—that to spare them, he did not spare himself. He must assuredly have burned with a wonderful and more than human zeal, inasmuch as, along with the labor of teaching, he labored with his own hands to earn a livelihood and in this respect refrained from exercising his right. For it is the law of Christ, as the apostle teaches elsewhere (see 1 Corinthians 9:14), that every church furnish its ministers with food and other necessities. Paul, therefore, in laying no burden on the Thessalonians, did something more than his office required of him. In addition to this, he did not merely refrain from incurring public expense but avoided burdening anyone individually. Further, there can be no doubt that he was influenced by some good and special consideration in thus refraining from exercising his right among the Thessalonians, for in other churches he exercised the freedom allowed him, just as other people did. However, he received nothing from the Corinthians, lest he should give the false apostles a reason to glory in this matter.

In the meantime, he did not hesitate to ask from other churches what was needed by him, for he writes that while he bestowed labor on the Corinthians free of charge, he accepted money from the churches that he did not serve (see 2 Corinthians 11:8). Hence, although the reason is not stated here, we may nevertheless conjecture that the ground on which Paul was unwilling that his necessities should be ministered to was lest such a thing should put any hindrance in the way of the Gospel. This also ought to be a matter of concern to good pastors—that they may not merely run with alacrity in their ministry, but may, so far as is in their power, remove all hindrances in the way of their course.

10. You are witnesses. The apostle again calls God and them to witness, with the view of affirming his integrity, and cites on the one hand God as a witness of his conscience, and the Thessalonians on the other hand as witnesses of what they had known by experience. **How holy**, he says, and **righteous . . . we were among you**—that is, with how sincere a fear of God and with what faithfulness and blamelessness toward men. By **blameless** he means he had given no occasion of complaint. Christ's servants cannot avoid false accusations and unfavorable reports, for being hated by the world, they must of necessity be spoken evil of among the wicked. Hence the apostle restricts this to those **who believed**, who judge uprightly and sincerely and do not revile malignantly and groundlessly.

11. He insists more especially on those things that belong to his office. He has compared himself to a nursing mother, and now he compares himself to a **father**. What he means is that he was concerned about them just as a father is concerned about his children over whom he exercises paternal care by teaching and admonishing. Unquestionably, no one will ever be a good pastor unless he shows himself to be a father to the church that is committed to him. Nor does he merely declare himself to be such to the whole body of the church there, but also to the individual members. It is not enough that a pastor in the pulpit teaches everyone together, if he does not add also particular instruction as necessity requires or as the occasion offers. Hence Paul himself, in Acts 20:26, declares himself to be innocent of the blood of all men because he did not cease to admonish everyone publicly and also individuals in the privacy of their own homes. We must remember that instruction given to everyone together is sometimes of little benefit, and some persons cannot be corrected or cured without particular medicine.

12. Encouraging. The apostle shows with what earnestness he devoted himself to the Thessalonian believers' welfare, for he relates that in preaching to them about piety toward God and the duties of the Christian life, it had not been merely in a perfunctory way; rather, he says he had made use of exhortations. It is a living preaching of the Gospel when people are not merely told what is right but have their consciences pricked (see Acts 2:37) by exhortations and are called to God's judgment seat, that they may not fall asleep in their vices. But if pious people, whose prompt obedience Paul so highly commends, needed to be stimulated by stirring exhortations, what must be done with us in whom indolence and negligence of the flesh reign? Concerning the wicked, whose obstinacy is incurable, it is necessary to proclaim to them the horrible vengeance of God, not merely in hope of success, but so they may have no excuse.

Comforting. The apostle may mean that he made use of consolations in dealing with the afflicted, those who need to be sustained by God's grace and refreshed by tasting the heavenly blessings, that they may not lose heart or become impatient. Another meaning, however, is more suitable to the context—that he "admonished," for the three verbs in this verse clearly refer to the same thing.

Urging you to live lives worthy of God. The apostle now presents in a few words the sum and substance of his exhortations; in magnifying the mercy of God, he admonishes them not to fail in their calling. His commendation of the grace of God is contained in the expression, **who calls you into his kingdom and glory.** As our salvation is founded on God's gracious adoption, every blessing that Christ has brought us is included in this one term. It is now up to us to answer God's call—that is, to show ourselves to be such children to him as he is a Father to us, for those who live other than as becomes children of God deserve to be cut off from God's household.

Verses 13-16

And we also thank God continually because, when you received the word of God, which you heard from us, you accepted it not as the word of men, but as it actually is, the word of God, which is at work in you who believe. For you, brothers, became imitators of God's churches in Judea, which are in Christ Jesus: You suffered from your own countrymen the same things those churches suffered from the Jews, who killed the Lord Jesus and the prophets and also drove us out. They displease God and are hostile to all men in their effort to keep us from speaking to the Gentiles so that they may be saved. In this way they always heap up their sins to the limit. The wrath of God has come upon them at last.

13. Having spoken of his ministry, the apostle returns again to address the Thessalonians, that he may always commend the mutual harmony that he'd mentioned. He says, therefore, that he gives thanks to God because they had **received the word of God** and because they had **accepted it not as the word of men, but as it actually is, the word of God**. By these expressions the apostle means that the Word had been received by them reverently and with the obedience it deserved. For as soon as this persuasion has gained a foothold, it is impossible not to have a spirit of obedience take possession of our minds. Who would not shudder at the thought of resisting God? Who would not regard contempt of God with detestation? Therefore, when the Word of God is regarded by many with contempt, when it is scarcely held in any estimation and many are not at all actuated by fear of God, it is because they do not consider they have anything to do with God or must answer to him.

Hence we learn from this passage what credit ought to be given to the Gospel—such as does not depend on human authority but, resting on the sure and ascertained truth of God, raises itself above the world and, in sum, is as far above mere opinion as heaven is above earth. Second, such an attitude produces reverence, fear, and obedience inasmuch as people, touched with a feeling of divine majesty, will never allow themselves to play games with it. Teachers are, in turn, admonished to beware of bringing forward anything but the pure Word of God, for if this was not allowable for Paul, it will not be so for anyone in the present day. He proves, however, from the effect produced that it was the Word of God that he had delivered, inasmuch as it had produced that fruit of heavenly doctrine that the prophets celebrated (see Isaiah 55:11, 13; Jeremiah 23:29), renewing and reforming the life of the Thessalonians. The Thessalonians felt in themselves the divine energy that proceeds from faith; they could rest assured that what they had heard was not a mere sound of the human voice vanishing into air, but the living and efficacious teaching of God.

As for the expression **the word of God**, it simply means "the Word of God preached by man." Paul meant to state expressly that they had not looked on the doctrine as contemptible, although it had proceeded from the mouth of a mortal, for they recognized God as its author. The apostle accordingly praised the Thessalonians because they did not rest in mere regard for the minister but lifted up their eyes to God, that they might receive his word.

14. For you, brothers, became imitators. If you are inclined to restrict this to the clause immediately linked to it, the meaning will be that the power of God, or of his Word, showed itself in their patient endurance as they bore persecution with magnanimity and undaunted courage. I prefer, however, to view it as extending to the whole of the previous statement, for he confirms what he has stated, that the Thessalonians had in good earnest welcomed the Gospel as being presented to them by God, inasmuch as they courageously endured the assaults Satan made on them and did not refuse to suffer anything rather than not obey it. Unquestionably, it is no slight test of faith when Satan, by all his machinations, has no success in moving us away from the fear of God.

In the meantime, the apostle prudently provided against a dangerous temptation that might harass them, for they endured grievous troubles from the nation that was the only one in the world that gloried in the name of God. This, I say, might occur to their minds: "If this gospel is true religion, why do the Jews, who are the sacred people of God, oppose it with such inveterate hostility?" In order to remove this occasion of offense to the Thessalonians, the apostle, in the first place, showed them that they had this in common with the first **churches in Judea**, and later he says that the Jews are determined enemies of God and of all sound doctrine. When he says they suffered from their **own countrymen,** he may have been referring to others rather than to the Jews, or at least it ought not to be restricted to the Jews exclusively. Yet as he describes their obstinacy and impiety, it is clear that from the outset he has been speaking about these same people. Some of that nation had probably been converted to Christ at Thessalonica. It appears, however, from the narrative in Acts that there, no less than in Judea, the Jews were persecutors of the Gospel. I accordingly take this statement as being said indiscriminately of Jews as well as of Gentiles, inasmuch as both endured great conflicts and fierce attacks from their **own countrymen.**

15. Who killed the Lord Jesus. As that people had been distinguished by so many benefits from God, in consequence of the glory of the ancient fathers, the very name of *Jew* was of great authority among them. Lest this disguise should dazzle anyone's eyes, the apostle strips the Jews of all honor, so as to leave them nothing but odium and the utmost infamy. "Behold," he says, "the virtues for which they deserve praise among the good and pious! They killed their own prophets and at last the Son of God, and they have persecuted me, his servant. They wage war with God, they are detested by the whole world, they are hostile to the salvation of the Gentiles; in short, they are destined to everlasting destruction." Why does the apostle say that Christ and **the prophets** were killed by the same people? This refers to the entire body of people, for Paul means there is nothing new or unusual in their resisting God, but that on the contrary they are in this manner filling up the measure of the sin of their fathers, just as Christ had said (see Matthew 23:32).

16. To keep us from speaking to the Gentiles. The apostle has good reason for entering into so much detail in exposing the malice of the Jews. For as they furiously opposed the Gospel everywhere, there arose from this a great stumbling-block, especially as they exclaimed that the Gospel was profaned by Paul when he made it known among the Gentiles. By this calumny they divided the churches, they took away from the Gentiles the hope of salvation, and they put obstacles in the path of the Gospel. Paul, accordingly, charged them regarding the salvation of the Gentiles with envy, adding that matters were so in order that they might **heap up their sins to the limit**, taking away from them all reputation for piety, just as in saying previously that **they displease God** (verse 15), he meant they were unworthy to be reckoned among the worshipers of God. This expression about heaping up their sins implies that those who persevere in an evil course fill up by this means the measure of their judgment and condemnation, until they come under God's final wrath. This is the reason why the punishment of the wicked is often delayed—because their impieties, so to speak, are not yet ripe. By this we are warned that we must carefully take heed lest, in the event of our adding from time to time sin to sin, the heap at last reaches as high as heaven.

The wrath of God has come. The apostle means that they were in an utterly hopeless state, inasmuch as they were vessels of the Lord's wrath. "The just vengeance of God presses upon them and pursues them and will not leave them until they perish—as is the case with all the reprobate, who rush on headlong to death, for which they are destined." The apostle, however, makes this declaration regarding the entire body of the people in such a manner as not to deprive the elect of hope. As the greater proportion resisted Christ, he speaks, it is true, of the whole nation generally; but we must keep in view the exception that he himself cited in Romans 11:5—that the Lord will always have some seed remaining. We must always keep in view Paul's design—that believers must carefully avoid the society of those whom the just vengeance of God pursues until they perish in their blind obstinacy. **Wrath**, without any additional term, means the judgment of God, as in Romans 4:15, "law brings wrath"; also in Romans 12:19, "leave room for God's wrath."

Verses 17-20

But, brothers, when we were torn away from you for a short time (in person, not in thought), out of our intense longing we made every effort to see you. For we wanted to come to you—certainly I, Paul, did, again and again—but Satan stopped us. For what is our hope, our joy, or the crown in which we will glory in the presence of our Lord Jesus when he comes? Is it not you? Indeed, you are our glory and joy.

17. This was added lest the Thessalonians should think Paul had deserted them when so great an emergency demanded his presence. He had spoken of the persecutions they endured from their own people; he in the meantime whose duty it was above all others to assist them was absent. He has already called himself a father; it is not the part of a father to desert his children in the midst of such distresses. He, accordingly, obviates all

suspicion of contempt and negligence by saying that it was from no want of inclination but because he had no opportunity. Nor does he say simply, "I was desirous to come to you, but my way was obstructed"; rather, by the peculiar terms he uses he expresses the intensity of his affection: "When I was bereaved of you." He thus declares how sad and distressing a thing it was to him to be absent from them. This is followed by a fuller expression of his feelings—that it was only with difficulty that he could endure their absence for a short time. **We were torn away from you for a short time.** It is no surprise if long length of time should bring weariness or sadness; but we must have a strong feeling of attachment when we find it difficult to wait even a single hour.

This is followed by an amplification—he had been separated from them **in person, not in thought**, so they would know that distance of place did not by any means lessen his attachment. At the same time, this might no less appropriately be applied to the Thessalonians as meaning that they, for their part, had felt united in mind while absent in body; for it was of no small importance for the point in hand that he should state how fully assured he was of their affection toward him in return. However, he shows his affection more fully when he says that he **made every effort to see** them, meaning that his affection was not diminished by his leaving them but had been the more inflamed. When he says, **we wanted to come to you** (verse 18), he declares that it was not a sudden heat that quickly cooled (as we see sometimes happen), but that he had been steadfast in this purpose, inasmuch as he sought various opportunities.

18. Satan stopped us. Luke relates that Paul was in one instance hindered (Acts 20:3), inasmuch as the Jews laid an ambush for him along the route he traveled. The same thing, or something similar, may have occurred frequently. It is not without good reason, however, that Paul ascribes the whole of this to Satan, for as he teaches elsewhere (Ephesians 6:12), we have to wrestle not against flesh and blood but against principalities and spiritual wickedness. Whenever the wicked molest us, they fight under Satan's banner and are his instruments for harassing us. More especially, when our endeavors are directed to the work of the Lord, it is certain that everything that hinders us proceeds in some way from Satan. If only this sentiment were deeply impressed upon the minds of all pious people—that Satan is continually contriving, by every means, in whatever way he can hinder or obstruct the edification of the church! We would then assuredly be more careful to resist him; we would take more care to maintain sound teaching, of which that enemy strives so keenly to deprive us. We would also, whenever the course of the Gospel is retarded, know from where the hindrance proceeds. Paul says elsewhere (Acts 16:7) that *God* had not permitted him, but both were true, for although Satan does his part, yet God retains supreme authority and opens a way for us as often as he sees good, against Satan's will and in spite of his opposition. Paul accordingly says truly that God does not permit, although the hindrance comes from Satan.

19. For what is our hope . . . ? The apostle confirms that ardor of desire he had often mentioned inasmuch as he has his happiness in a manner treasured up in them. "Unless I forget myself, I must necessarily desire your presence, for **you are our glory and joy.**" Further, when he calls them his **hope . . . the crown in which we will glory,** we must not understand this as meaning that he gloried in anyone except God alone, because we are allowed to glory in all God's favors, in their own place, in such a way that he is always our desire. We must, however, infer from this that Christ's ministers will on the last day, as they have individually promoted his kingdom, take part in glory and triumph. Let them therefore now learn to rejoice and glory in nothing but the prosperous issue of their labors when they see that the glory of Christ is promoted by their instrumentality. The consequence will be that they will be actuated by a spirit of affection to the church as they ought.

1 Thessalonians
Chapter 3

Verses 1-5

So when we could stand it no longer, we thought it best to be left by ourselves in Athens. We sent Timothy, who is our brother and God's fellow worker in spreading the gospel of Christ, to strengthen and encourage you in your faith, so that no one would be unsettled by these trials. You know quite well that we were destined for them. In fact, when we were with you, we kept telling you that we would be persecuted. And it turned out that way, as you well know. For this reason, when I could stand it no longer, I sent to find out about your faith. I was afraid that in some way the tempter might have tempted you and our efforts might have been useless.

1. By the detail that follows, the apostle assures them of the desire of which he had spoken. For if, being detained elsewhere, he had sent nobody else to Thessalonica in his place, it might have seemed as though he were not concerned about them so much; but by substituting Timothy for himself, he removed that suspicion. He showed that he esteemed them above himself in that he chose to be left alone rather than that they should be deserted. For the words, **so when we could stand it no longer**, are emphatic. Timothy was a most faithful companion to Paul; the apostle had at that time no others with him. Hence it was inconvenient and distressing for him to be without Timothy. It was therefore a token of rare affection and anxious desire that he did not refuse to deprive himself of this comfort in order to relieve the Thessalonians. To the same effect the words **we thought it best** express a prompt inclination of the mind.

2. Our brother. The apostle assigned to Timothy marks of commendation, that he might show more clearly how much he cared about the Thessalonians' welfare. If he had sent them some common person, that would not have afforded them much assistance. And if Paul would have done this without inconveniencing himself, he would have given no remarkable proof of his fatherly concern about the Thessalonians. He did a great thing by depriving himself of a **brother** and **fellow worker**, one whose equal he had not found, as he declared in Philippians 2:20-21, since everyone else sought their own interests. By speaking in this way, Paul validated the authority of the teaching they had received from Timothy, so it would remain more deeply impressed on their memory.

However, the apostle has an additional good reason for saying he had **sent Timothy** so they might receive strength and encouragement in their **faith** from Paul's own example. They might be intimidated by unpleasant reports about persecutions, but the apostle's undaunted constancy so animated them that they did not give up. In the fellowship of the saints, the faith of one is a consolation for others. Hearing that Paul was going on with indefatigable zeal and was with faith surmounting all dangers and all difficulties and that his faith continued everywhere victorious against Satan and the world brought the Thessalonians no small encouragement. We are, or at least ought to be, stimulated by the examples of those by whom we were instructed in the faith, as is stated at the end of the letter to the Hebrews: "Remember your leaders, who spoke the word of God to you" (13:7). Paul meant in 1 Thessalonians 3 that they ought to be fortified by his example, so as not to give way under their afflictions. As, however, they might have been offended if Paul had expressed a fear that they might all give way under persecution (since this would evidence excessive distrust), he mitigates this harshness by saying, "so that no one" (verse 3). There was, however, good reason to fear such a fall, as there are weak people in every society and church.

3. You know quite well. Though all would gladly exempt themselves from the necessity of bearing the cross, Paul teaches that there is no reason why believers should feel dismayed when they face persecutions, as though it were a thing that was new and unusual, inasmuch as this is the situation the Lord has assigned to us. Concerning the expression **that we were destined for them**, it is as though he said that this is inseparable from our being Christians. The apostle says they **know** it, and so it became them to fight more valiantly and courageously, for they had been forewarned in time. In addition to this, incessant afflictions made Paul contemptible among rude and ignorant people. But he stated that nothing had befallen him but what he had long before, in the manner of a prophet, foretold.

5. In some way the tempter might have tempted you. The apostle teaches us that temptations are always to be dreaded, because it is Satan's function to entice us to evil. He never ceases to ambush us on all sides and to lay snares for us everywhere; so we must be on our watch, eagerly keeping alert. And now he says openly what at the outset he had avoided saying, since it was so harsh—that he had felt concerned lest his **efforts might**

have been useless, which would be the case if Satan had managed to prevail. The apostle states this so that they may keep careful watch and may stir themselves up even more vigorously to resistance.

Verses 6-10

But Timothy has just now come to us from you and has brought good news about your faith and love. He has told us that you always have pleasant memories of us and that you long to see us, just as we also long to see you. Therefore, brothers, in all our distress and persecution we were encouraged about you because of your faith. For now we really live, since you are standing firm in the Lord. How can we thank God enough for you in return for all the joy we have in the presence of our God because of you? Night and day we pray most earnestly that we may see you again and supply what is lacking in your faith.

The apostle showed here, by another argument, his extraordinary affection toward them, inasmuch as he was overjoyed by their being in a prosperous condition. We must take notice of his circumstances at that time. He was in distress and was being persecuted. There might have seemed to be no room for cheerfulness. But when he heard about the reality of what he so much desired for the Thessalonians, all feelings of distress seemed to vanish, and he experienced great joy. He expressed the greatness of his joy in degrees. He says in the first place, **we were encouraged** (verse 7). Later he speaks of a joy that was plentifully poured out (verse 9). This manner of testifying to the joy he felt about the steadfastness of the Thessalonians had the force of an exhortation, for Paul's intention was to stir up the Thessalonians to persevere. It was undoubtedly a most powerful encouragement when they learned that the holy apostle felt so great consolation and joy from the progress they had made in their piety.

6. Faith and love. This form of expression should be carefully observed because of the frequency with which Paul uses it. In these two words he comprehends briefly the sum of true piety. Hence all who aim at this twofold mark, as long as they do so, will not fall into error. All others wander miserably.

8. For now we really live. Here it appears even more clearly that Paul almost forgot himself for the sake of the Thessalonians or regarded himself secondarily, devoting his first and chief thoughts to them. He did not do that so much out of affection to men as from a desire for the Lord's glory. Zeal for God and Christ resided in him to such a degree that it in some manner swallowed up all other anxieties. **We really live,** he says; that is, "we are in good health if you **stand firm in the Lord.**" By the adverb **now** he was hinting at what he had formerly stated, that previously he had been greatly pressed down by **distress** and **persecution.** Yet he declared that whatever evil he endured in his own person did not hinder his joy. "Though in myself I am dead, yet in your welfare I live." All pastors can learn from this what kind of link should exist between them and the church—they can reckon themselves happy when it goes well with the church, even if they are in other respects surrounded with many miseries; conversely, they pine away with grief if they see the church they have built in a state of decay, even if matters otherwise are joyful and prosperous.

9. Not satisfied with a simple affirmation, the apostle next intimated how extraordinary was the greatness of his joy by asking himself, **How can we thank God enough for you . . . ?** By speaking in this way he declared that he could not find an expression of gratitude that could come up to the measure of his joy. He said that he rejoiced **in the presence of our God**—that is, truly and without any pretense.

10. **Night and day we pray most earnestly.** The apostle then returned to an expression of his desire. It is never allowable for us to congratulate people while they live in this world in such unqualified terms as not always to desire something better for them. They are still on the way; they may fall back or go astray. Hence Paul is eager for an opportunity to **supply what is lacking in your faith** or, which is the same thing, to complete their faith, which was as yet imperfect. Now, this is the faith he had previously extolled. From this we infer that those who far surpass others are still far away from the goal. Hence, whatever progress we may have made, let us always keep in view our deficiencies, that we may not be reluctant to aim at something higher.

From this also it appears how necessary it is for us to give careful attention to teaching the Christian faith, for teachers and others who have the task of instructing in the church were not appointed merely to lead men and women to faith in Christ for a single day or month but to perfect the faith that had been begun. His saying that he prayed **night and day** shows how persistent he was in praying to God for the Thessalonians, and with what ardor and earnestness he discharged that duty.

Verses 11-13

Now may our God and Father himself and our Lord Jesus clear the way for us to come to you. May the Lord make your love increase and overflow for each other and for everyone else, just as ours does for you. May he strengthen your hearts so that you will be blameless and holy in the presence of our God and Father when our Lord Jesus comes with all his holy ones.

11. The apostle now prays that the Lord, removing Satan's obstructions, will open a door for him to be, as it were, a leader to the Thessalonians. By this he intimates that we cannot move a step that will be

profitable or prosperous unless it is under God's guidance. But when God is with us, it does not matter if Satan employs every effort he can to change the direction we are taking. We must take notice that Paul credits the same role to God and to Christ; unquestionably, the Father confers no blessing upon us except through Christ's hand. Moreover, when he speaks of both in the same terms, he teaches that Christ has divinity and power in common with the Father.

12. May the Lord make your love increase and overflow. Here Paul prays that while his way is obstructed and he is absent from them, the Lord will confirm the Thessalonians in holiness and fill them with love. From this we learn what the perfection of the Christian life consists of — love and pure holiness of heart, flowing from faith. He recommends love mutually cherished — **for each other** — and afterwards **for everyone else.** As it is fitting that we should be made one with those who are of the household of faith (see Galatians 6:10), so our love should also go out to the whole human race. The nearer connection must be cherished, but we must not overlook those who are more distant from us.

The apostle wanted the Thessalonians to abound in love and be filled with it, because insofar as we make progress in our relationship with God, the love of the brethren will certainly at the same time increase in us, until it captures our whole heart, with the corrupt love of self being driven out. He prayed that the love of the Thessalonians would be made perfect by God, intimating that its increase, no less than its commencement, was from God alone. Hence it is evident how preposterous a part those act who measure their strength by their ability to keep the precepts of the divine law. Indeed, "the goal of this command is love" (1 Timothy 1:5). But as Paul himself declared, love is a work of God, not of us. When God marks out our faults and infirmities, he does not look to what we can do but requires from us what is above our strength, that we may learn to ask from him the power to accomplish it. When the apostle says, **just as ours does for you,** he stimulates them by his own example.

13. May he strengthen your hearts. The apostle used the term **hearts** here to mean the conscience or the innermost part of the soul. He meant that a person is acceptable to God (**blameless and holy**) only when he has holiness of heart — that is, not external, but internal. Is it by means of holiness that we stand at God's judgment seat, and if so, what good does remission of sins serve? Paul's words seem to imply that their consciences might be beyond reproach because of their holiness. But Paul did not exclude remission of sins, through which our holiness, which is otherwise polluted, receives God's approval. Faith, by which God is pacified toward us and pardons our faults, precedes everything else, just as the foundation is laid before the building is erected. Paul, however, did not teach us what or how great the holiness of believers may be but desired that it may be increased until it attains perfection. On this account he said, **when our Lord Jesus comes,** meaning that the completion of those things that the Lord has begun in us is delayed until that time.

With all his holy ones. This clause may be explained in two ways, either as meaning that the Thessalonians may have pure hearts **with all his holy ones** at Christ's coming, or that Christ will come **with all his holy ones.** While I adopt this second meaning, insofar as the construction of the words suggests this, I have at the same time no doubt that Paul used this term **holy ones** for the purpose of admonishing us that we are called by Christ so that we may be gathered **with all his holy ones.** This consideration ought to whet our desire for holiness.

1 Thessalonians
Chapter 4

Verses 1-5

Finally, brothers, we instructed you how to live in order to please God, as in fact you are living. Now we ask you and urge you in the Lord Jesus to do this more and more. For you know what instructions we gave you by the authority of the Lord Jesus. It is God's will that you should be sanctified: that you should avoid sexual immorality; that each of you should learn to control his own body in a way that is holy and honorable, not in passionate lust like the heathen, who do not know God.

1. This chapter contains various injunctions by which the apostle trained the Thessalonians to live a holy life or confirmed them in their exercise of it. They had previously learned the rule and the method of a pious life, and the apostle calls this to mind. "As," he says in effect, "you have been taught." Lest, however, he should seem to take away from them what he had previously assigned to them, he does not simply exhort them **to live** in a certain way but **to do this more and more.** When, therefore, he urges them to make progress, he intimates that they are already doing the right thing. In sum, they should be especially careful to make progress in the teaching they had received, and this Paul contrasts with frivolous and vain pursuits, in which a good part of the world generally busies itself, so that profitable and holy meditation scarcely obtains a place.

Paul accordingly reminds them in what manner they had been instructed and bids them aim at this with all their strength. "Forgetting what is behind" (Philippians 3:13), we must always aim to make more progress, and pastors should also make this their aim. As to Paul's **urging** when he could have rightfully given a command, this is a token of humanity and modesty that pastors should imitate—namely, if possible, allure people to kindness rather than force them rudely and in a violent manner.

3. It is God's will that you should be sanctified. This is teaching of a general nature from which, as from a fountain, the apostle immediately deduces special admonitions. When he says, **it is God's will,** he means we have been called by God for this purpose. "For this end you are Christians—this is what the Gospel aims at—that you may be holy before God." The meaning of the word **holy** or **sanctification** (KJV) is renouncing the world, clearing out the pollutions of the flesh, and offering ourselves to God in sacrifice, for nothing can with propriety be offered to him but what is pure and holy.

That you should avoid sexual immorality. The apostle derived this command from the fountain he had just mentioned, for nothing is more against holiness than the defilement of **sexual immorality,** which pollutes the whole person. On this account he assigns **passionate lust** to **the heathen, who do not know God** (verse 5). Where the knowledge of God reigns, lusts will be subdued.

By **sexual immorality** the apostle meant all base desires of the flesh, but by this expression he also branded with dishonor all desires that allure us to earthly pleasures and delights. "Rather, clothe yourselves with the Lord Jesus Christ, and do not think about how to gratify the desires of the sinful nature" (Romans 13:14). When men indulge their appetites, there is no end to their debauchery and wantonness. Hence, the only way to maintain temperance is to bridle all base desires.

4. That each of you should learn to control his own body. Some people explain these words as referring to a wife in relation to her husband, as though Paul was saying, "Let husbands live with their wives in complete chastity." As, however, he addressed husbands and wives indiscriminately, there can be no doubt that he is talking about a person's own body, for everyone has a body as a sort of house to live in. The apostle would, therefore, have us all, whether married or not, keep our body pure from all uncleanness—**in a way that is holy.**

And honorable. Anyone who prostitutes the body with sexual immorality covers it with infamy and disgrace.

Verses 6-8

And that in this matter no one should wrong his brother or take advantage of him. The Lord will punish men for all such sins, as we have already told you and warned you. For God did not call us to be impure, but to live a holy life. Therefore, he who rejects this instruction does not reject man but God, who gives you his Holy Spirit.

6. Here we have another exhortation that flows like a stream from the teaching about sanctification. "God," Paul said, "has it in view to sanctify us, so that **no one should wrong his brother or take advantage of him.**" Chrysostom's linking this statement with the preceding one and explaining **no one should wrong . . . or take advantage of** to mean "neighing for another man's wife" (Jeremiah 5:8) and eagerly desiring her is too forced an exposition. Paul, having adduced one instance of unchastity concerning lust, now teaches that another part of holiness is to behave ourselves righteously and harmlessly toward our neighbors. **No one should wrong** refers to violent oppressions, when the man who has more power is so bold that he inflicts injury. **Take advantage of** includes all immoderate and unrighteous desires. As, however, men for the most part indulge themselves in lust and avarice, he reminds them of what he had previously taught—**the Lord will punish men for all such sins**. We must observe also what he added: **as we have already told you and warned you.** Human beings are so sluggish that unless they are wounded deeply, they have no understanding about God's judgment.

7. **For God did not call us to be impure, but to live a holy life.** This appears to be the same thought as the preceding one—that the will of God is for us to be sanctified or holy. There is, however, a little difference between them. Having spoken about correcting the vices of the flesh, he demonstrates from the purpose of our calling that God desires this; he sets us apart for himself as his special possession. Paul now uses a contrasting illustration to demonstrate God's calling us to holiness—he rescues us and calls us back from unchastity. From this the apostle concludes that all who reject this teaching do **not reject man but God** (verse 8), the Author of this calling. The reason the apostle became so vehement is because there are always base people who fearlessly despise God, ridicule all talk about his judgment, and treat with contempt all commands to live a holy and pious life. Such people cannot be taught but must be withstood and fervently opposed.

8. **Who gives you his Holy Spirit.** In order to press the point home to the Thessalonians that they must turn away from such contempt and obstinacy, the apostle reminded them that they had been endowed with the Spirit of God. He did this, first, so they could identify what comes from God; second, so they could distinguish between holiness and impurity; and, third, so, with heavenly authority, they could pronounce judgment against all sexual immorality—which they would be engulfed in if they did not take steps to avoid being contaminated. Wicked men may ridicule all instructions that are given about a holy life and the fear of God. But people who are endowed with God's Spirit have a very different testimony sealed on their hearts. We must therefore take heed that we do not ignore or silence him. At the same time, Paul may be saying here that it is

not from any human viewpoint that they are to condemn sexual immorality, but with God's authority. I am inclined to include both meanings.

Verses 9-12

Now about brotherly love we do not need to write to you, for you yourselves have been taught by God to love each other. And in fact, you do love all the brothers throughout Macedonia. Yet we urge you, brothers, to do so more and more. Make it your ambition to lead a quiet life, to mind your own business and to work with your hands, just as we told you, so that your daily life may win the respect of outsiders and so that you will not be dependent on anybody.

9. Now about brotherly love. Having previously, in lofty terms, commended their love, he now spoke by way of anticipation, saying, **we do not need to write to you.** He gave a reason—**for you yourselves have been taught by God**—by which he means that since love was engraved on their hearts, there was no need for further instruction written on paper. He does not just mean what John writes about in his first letter: "As for you, the anointing you received from him remains in you, and you do not need anyone to teach you. But as his anointing teaches you about all things and as that anointing is real, not counterfeit—just as it has taught you, remain in him" (1 John 2:27). Their hearts were saturated with love, showing that the Holy Spirit had inwardly dictated efficaciously what should be done, so that there was no need to given written instructions. In this argument Paul moved from the greater to the lesser. Since their love diffused itself throughout the whole of Macedonia, he inferred that there was no doubt that they did indeed **love each other.** The conjunction **for** means "likewise." He added this for greater emphasis.

10. Yet we urge you. Although the apostle declared that the Thessalonians were sufficiently prepared for all ministries of love, he nevertheless did not cease to exhort them to make progress, for no one in this life has reached perfection. Unquestionably, even if we appear to be making excellent progress, we must still desire to become even better. Some link the verb **make it your ambition** (verse 11) with what follows, as if he exhorted them to strive to keep the peace; but it goes better with the previous sentence. After he admonished them to increase in love, he told them to each strive to be victorious in the matter of mutual affection. In order that their love may be perfect or complete, the apostle said there should be a great effort made among them, just as there is among those who are seeking to win a victory in battle.

11. Lead a quiet life. This means to act peacefully and without disturbance—as we say in French, *sans bruit* (without noise). In short, the apostle exhorted them to be peaceable and tranquil, **to mind your own**

business. We commonly see that those who intrude into other people's affairs create a great disturbance and make trouble for others as well as for themselves. The best way to lead a tranquil life is for all to be absorbed with the duties of their own calling, carrying out the duties given them by the Lord and devoting themselves to these things. The farmer concentrates on his rural activities, the workman busily carries out his labors, and so on, and in this way everyone keeps within their own boundaries. But as soon as people turn away from this, everything is thrown into confusion and disorder. The apostle does not mean, however, that everyone should **mind [their] own business** in such a way that they all live separate lives and do not care for one another.

Work with your hands. The apostle recommends manual labor for two reasons (verse 12). First, so they would have enough money to live on; and, second, so they would live in an honorable way in front of unbelievers. Nothing is more offensive than a person who is an idle good-for-nothing, who benefits neither himself nor anybody else, and who appears to have been born just to eat and drink. In addition, this truth has a further application, for what the apostle says about hands is a synecdoche; he clearly includes every useful employment of human life.

Verses 13-14

Brothers, we do not want you to be ignorant about those who fall asleep, or to grieve like the rest of men, who have no hope. We believe that Jesus died and rose again and so we believe that God will bring with Jesus those who have fallen asleep in him.

13. Brothers, we do not want you to be ignorant about those who fall asleep. It is unlikely that the hope of a resurrection had been spread among the Thessalonians by ungodly men, as was the case in Corinth. The apostle rebuked the Corinthians severely, but here he referred to the resurrection as a thing that was not in doubt. It is possible, however, that this conviction was not strong enough in the Thessalonian believers' minds and that they, mourning for the dead, retained part of their old superstitions. The sum of the whole passage is this—we must not grieve for the dead beyond certain bounds, for all God's children are going to be raised again. The mourning of unbelievers knows no bounds because they have no hope in the resurrection. The apostle will later teach about the resurrection, and he will also say something about when this will take place; but in this passage he simply intends to curb excessive grief, which would never have happened among them if they had seriously considered the resurrection and kept it in the forefront of their minds.

The apostle did not, however, forbid us to mourn at all; rather, he wanted our mourning to be within the bounds of moderation, for we are not **to grieve like the rest of men, who have no hope.** The apostle forbade the Thessalonians to grieve like unbelievers, who give full rein to their grief because they view death as the final destruction and imagine that everything removed from this world perishes. Since, on the other hand, believers know that when they leave this world they will finally be gathered into God's kingdom, they have no reason for undue grief. Knowledge of the resurrection is good reason for grieving in moderation.

The apostle refers to the dead as **those who fall asleep,** a term in which the bitterness of death is mitigated, for there is a great deal of difference between sleeping and being reduced to nothing and being destroyed. However, this does not refer to the soul but to the body, for the dead body lies in the grave until God raises it up. Therefore, those who infer from this that souls sleep are very foolish.

Paul lifts up the minds of believers to consider the resurrection in case they should indulge in excessive grief at the loss of a loved relative. People who abuse this testimony and make a class of stoics among Christians, who view everything with hard indifference, will find no comfort in these words of Paul. The grief of the pious is to be mixed with consolation, which will train them in patience. The hope of a blessed resurrection will bring this about.

14. We believe that Jesus died and rose again. The apostle assumed this axiom of our faith: Christ was raised from the dead that we might share in the same resurrection. From this he went on to infer that we will live with Christ eternally. This teaching, however, also stated in 1 Corinthians 15:13 ("If there is no resurrection of the dead, then not even Christ has been raised"), depends on another principle—that it was not for himself but for us that Christ died and rose again. Hence those who have doubts about the resurrection do a great injustice to Christ. More than that, they in a way drag Christ down from heaven, as is said in Romans 10:6: "But the righteousness that is by faith says: 'Do not say in your heart, "Who will ascend into heaven?"' (that is, to bring Christ down)."

Have fallen asleep in him [Jesus]. We retain in death the link we have in Christ, for those who are by faith grafted into Christ have death in common with him so that they may take part in life with him. However, if it is asked if unbelievers will not also rise again, it should be noted that Paul does not here teach anything except what is appropriate for his present purpose, which is to correct the excessive grief of pious Christians, which he does with the medicine of consolation.

Verses 15-18

According to the Lord's own word, we tell you that we who are still alive, who are left till the coming of the Lord, will certainly not precede

those who have fallen asleep. **For the Lord himself will come down from heaven, with a loud command, with the voice of the archangel and with the trumpet call of God, and the dead in Christ will rise first. After that, we who are still alive and are left will be caught up with them in the clouds to meet the Lord in the air. And so we will be with the Lord forever. Therefore encourage each other with these words.**

15. The apostle now briefly explains the way in which believers will be raised up from death. As he speaks about a great thing that is incredible to the human mind and also promises what is beyond the power and choice of men, he states that he does not bring forward anything that stems from human reasoning, but rather the Lord is its author. It is probable that **the Lord's own word** means what was taken from Christ's discourses. Although Paul had learned by revelation the secrets of the heavenly kingdom, it was nevertheless more appropriate to fix in the minds of believers the belief in a resurrection by speaking about those things that had been uttered by Christ himself. "We are not the first witnesses of the resurrection—the Master himself has declared it. He affirmed it and testified to it in his discourses."

We who are still alive . . . will certainly not precede those who have fallen asleep. The apostle stated this so the Thessalonians would not think that only those alive at the time of Christ's coming would share in eternal life, that those who had already died would have no part in it. "The order of the resurrection," Paul says in effect, "will begin with those who have already departed; and we shall not rise without them." From this it is clear that a belief in a final resurrection had been, in some of their minds, obscure and mixed up with various erroneous ideas, inasmuch as they imagined that eternal life only belonged to those alive at Christ's final coming. Paul, to correct this error, assigned the first place to the dead and taught that those who are still alive will follow.

Paul was speaking in the first person and so put himself, as it were, among those who will be alive at the last day. He did this to arouse the Thessalonians to wait for this last day. In addition, Paul taught this doctrine so they would be prepared for Christ's return at any time. In the meantime, it was necessary to put a stop to all their idle curiosity, which the apostle did at even greater length later on. When, however, he said, **we who are still alive,** he made use of the present tense instead of the future, in accordance with the Hebrew idiom.

16. For the Lord himself will come down from heaven. Paul used the words **a loud command** (a shout) and then added, **with the voice of the archangel** by way of explanation, showing what kind of command will be given. The archangel will act as the herald to summon the living and the dead to Christ's tribunal. Although this will be common to all unfallen angels, yet, as is customary among different ranks, God appoints one to be the leader of the others. Regarding **the trumpet call**, the apostle unquestionably had nothing more in view here than to give some flavor of the magnificence and venerable appearance of the Judge, until we behold him fully. We should remain satisfied with this description for the time being.

The apostle then again says that **the dead in Christ will rise first**. So we know that the hope of life is laid up in heaven for them as well as for those who remain alive. The apostle says nothing about the reprobate; it is the pious about whom he is now speaking.

17. The apostle says that those who are alive at Christ's coming will **be caught up with them** (verse 17). These people will not experience death. Here Augustine finds a difficulty, mentioned both in the twentieth chapter of the *City of God* and in his *Answer to Dulcitius*, because Paul seems to contradict himself inasmuch as he says elsewhere, "What you sow does not come to life unless it dies" (1 Corinthians 15:36). However, a sudden change is like death. Ordinary death, it is true, is the separation of the soul from the body; but the Lord can in a moment destroy our corruptible nature and then create it anew by his power. This fits in with what Paul says elsewhere will take place — "that what is mortal may be swallowed up by life" (2 Corinthians 5:4). What is stated in our confession of faith, that "Christ will be the Judge of the dead and the living," Augustine acknowledges to be true. He is only at a loss about how those who have not died will rise again. But again, it is a kind of death when the flesh is reduced to nothing, for even now it is prone to corruption. The only difference is that those who are **asleep** put off the *substance* of the body for some space of time, but those who will be suddenly changed will put off the *quality*.

And so we will be with the Lord forever. Those who have already been gathered to Christ are promised eternal life with him. This statement totally refutes the fantasies of Origen and others. The life of believers, once they have been gathered into one kingdom, will have no end any more than Christ's. They will live with Christ as long as Christ himself exists.

18. **Encourage each other**. The apostle now shows more clearly that in the faith of the resurrection we have solid grounds for consolation, provided we are members of Christ and are truly united to him as our Head. At the same time, the apostle did not want each believer to merely seek for himself relief from grief but wanted them all to minister comfort to others as well.

1 Thessalonians
Chapter 5

Verses 1-5

Now, brothers, about times and dates we do not need to write to you, for you know very well that the day of the Lord will come like a thief in the night. While people are saying, "Peace and safety," destruction will come on them suddenly, as labor pains on a pregnant woman, and they will not escape. But you, brothers, are not in darkness so that this day should surprise you like a thief. You are all sons of the light and sons of the day. We do not belong to the night or to the darkness.

1. About times and dates. The apostle now recalled the Thessalonians from curious and unprofitable inquiry about **times** and at the same time urged them to be constantly in a state of preparation for receiving Christ when he comes to judge them. The apostle spoke, however, by way of anticipation, saying they did not need him to write about those things that the curious want to delve into. For it is proof of excessive incredulity not to believe what the Lord foretells unless he marks out the day by certain circumstances and, as it were, points it out with his finger. Those who require moments of time to be marked out for them are wavering between doubtful opinions, as if they want some clear proof of what they must believe. Paul said that discussions of this nature are not necessary for the pious. Believers should not desire to know more than they are permitted to learn in God's school. Christ planned that the day of his coming should be hidden from us, so that, being in suspense, we might remain on watch.

2. For you know very well that the day of the Lord will come like a thief in the night. The apostle contrasts exact knowledge with an anxious desire for investigation. But what is it that he says the Thessalonians know fully and for certain? It is that the day of Christ will come suddenly and unexpectedly and will take unbelievers by surprise, just as a thief does those who are asleep. This, however, is contrasted with clear signs that might indicate his coming was a long way off. Hence it is foolish to want to find out the precise time of Christ's coming from signs and portents.

3. Here we have an explanation of the similitude, **the day of the Lord will come like a thief in the night**. How is this? Because it will come suddenly to unbelievers, when it is not expected, so that they will be taken by surprise, as if they were sound asleep. But from where does that sleep come? Assuredly from their deep contempt for God. The prophets often reprove the wicked because of this negligence, and assuredly the ungodly wait in a spirit of carelessness not merely about the last judgment but also about everyday events that happen to them. Although the Lord threatens them with ruin and confusion, they do not hesitate to promise themselves peace and every kind of prosperity. The reason they fall into this indolence, which is so dangerous and deadly, is because they do not see that those things will take place soon. For this reason the Lord, in order that he may avenge this carelessness, which is full of obstinacy, arrives all of a sudden and against everyone's expectation. This brings about the fall of the wicked from their summit of felicity. The Lord sometimes furnishes tokens of the nature of this sudden coming, but the main one will be when Christ comes to judge he world, as he himself testified: "As it was in the days of Noah, so it will be at the coming of the Son of Man" (Matthew 24:37). Christ compared that time with the days of Noah inasmuch as all were given over to excess in their living, as if they were in the deepest sleep.

As labor pains on a pregnant woman. Here we have a most appropriate illustration, inasmuch as there is no pain that attacks more suddenly and that presses more keenly and violently. In addition to this, a woman who is with child carries in her womb the reason for the pains without feeling it until she is suddenly seized in the middle of feasting and laughter or in the middle of sleep.

4. But, you brothers. The apostle now admonishes the Thessalonians about their duty as believers as they look forward to the day of Christ's coming, even though it may be far off. This is what lies behind the metaphors of **darkness** and **day**. Christ's coming will surprise those who are living indulgent lives; because they are enclosed in darkness, they see nothing, for no darkness is as dense as ignorance of God. We, on the other hand, on whom Christ has shone by the faith of his Gospel, differ greatly from them. The saying in Isaiah is truly fulfilled in us: "See, darkness covers the earth and thick darkness is over the peoples, but the LORD rises upon you and his glory appears over you" (Isaiah 60:2). The apostle admonishes us, therefore, that it would be wrong for us to be caught by Christ sleeping, as it were, or seeing nothing when the full blaze of light is shining upon us.

5. You are all sons of the light and sons of the day. The apostle calls them children **of the light,** following the Hebrew idiom that means "furnished with light," and **sons of the day,** meaning "those who enjoy the light of day." Paul again emphasizes this when he says, **We do not belong to the night or to the darkness,** for the Lord has rescued us from it. We have not been enlightened by the Lord in order to walk in darkness.

Verses 6-10

So then, let us not be like others, who are asleep, but let us be alert and self-controlled. For those who sleep, sleep at night, and those who get drunk, get drunk at night. But since we belong to the day, let us be self-controlled, putting on faith and love as a breastplate, and the hope of salvation as a helmet. For God did not appoint us to suffer wrath but to receive salvation through our Lord Jesus Christ. He died for us so that, whether we are awake or asleep, we may live together with him.

6. So then, let us not be like others, who are asleep. The apostle now adds other metaphors closely linked to the preceding one. He had just shown how unacceptable it would be for believers to be blind in the middle of light, and now he points out that it would be dishonorable and disgraceful to sleep or be drunk in the middle of the day. He called the teaching of the Gospel **day** (verse 8), through which Christ, the Sun of righteousness (see Malachi 4:2), is manifested to us. When he spoke about sleep and drunkenness, he did not mean natural sleep or being drunk on wine, but the stupor of a mind that has forgotten God and has blindly indulged in vices. **Let us not be like others, who are asleep.** That is, let us not become sunken in indolence and senselessness in the world. **Like others**—that is, unbelievers, from whom ignorance of God, like a dark night, takes away understanding and reason. **But let us be alert.** That is, casting off the cares of the world, which burden us because of their weight, and throwing off base lusts, let us rise up to heaven with freedom and alacrity. It is spiritual sobriety when we use this world so sparingly and temperately that we are not entangled in its allurements.

8. Putting on faith and love as a breastplate. The apostle adds this in order to shake us more vehemently out of our stupor; he is, as it were, calling us to arms, demonstrating that this is not the time to sleep. It is true that he does not use the word *war*; but by arming us with **a breastplate** and a **helmet (the hope of salvation as a helmet),** the apostle is warning us that we must fight in a war. Whoever, therefore, is frightened of being surprised by the enemy must keep awake, so that he may constantly be on watch. The apostle has exhorted us to be vigilant on the grounds that the teaching of the Gospel is like the light of day, and now he stirs us up with another argument—we must wage war with our enemy. From this it follows that idleness is too much of a hazard to tolerate. Soldiers may be intemperate in other situations, but when the enemy is close, they fear for their lives, and so they refrain from gluttony, drunkenness, and all bodily pleasures and are constantly on their guard. As therefore Satan is always alert and seeking our downfall with his 1,001 schemes, should we not be at least as vigilant as soldiers are?

It is vain to seek too profound an exposition of the names of the different pieces of armor found here, for Paul here speaks in a different way from the way he does in Ephesians 6:14, where he makes righteousness the breastplate. To understand his meaning, it will therefore suffice to say that he wished to teach that the life of Christians is like a perpetual war, inasmuch as Satan does not cease to trouble and molest them. The apostle wants us to be properly prepared and fully alert in order to resist the enemy. Further, he admonishes us that we need arms because unless we are well-equipped, we will not be able to withstand so powerful and strong an enemy. He does not, however, enumerate all the parts of the armor but is content to mention just two of them—the **breastplate** and the **helmet**. At the same time, he omits nothing that belongs to spiritual armor, for the person who is provided with **faith**, **love**, and **hope** will not be unarmed in any way.

9. For God did not appoint us to suffer wrath. The apostle has spoken about **the hope of salvation** (verse 8) and now continues with this theme, saying that God has appointed us to **receive salvation through our Lord Jesus Christ**. This passage may be explained in the following way: we must put on the helmet of salvation because God does not will for us to perish but rather that we might be saved. This indeed is Paul's meaning, but in my opinion he had in mind something more. As the day of Christ is for the most part regarded with horror, and since the day of the Lord is thought of with dread, he says that we are **to receive salvation**.

Receive. Paul unquestionably does not mean that God has called us so we may procure or earn salvation for ourselves but rather that we may *obtain* it, for it has been acquired for us by Christ. Paul, however, encourages believers to fight strenuously, setting before them the certainty of victory, for the person who fights timidly is already half-defeated. With these words, therefore, the apostle intends to take away the dread that springs from distrust. There cannot, however, be a better assurance of salvation than what stems from God's decree and appointment. The term **wrath** in this passage, as in other instances, means the judgment or vengeance of God against reprobates.

10. He died for us. From the purpose of Christ's death, Paul confirms what he has said, for if Christ has died in order that we might share his life, there is no reason why we should entertain any doubts about our salvation. I am not certain what he means by **asleep** and **awake**, perhaps "life" and "death." Christ died to bestow on us his life, which is perpetual and has no end. It should not be thought strange, however, that he affirms that we now **live . . . with him [Christ]**, inasmuch as, entering through faith into the kingdom of Christ, we have passed from death to life (see John 5:24). Christ himself, into whose Body we are engrafted, makes us alive by his power, and the Spirit who lives in us is our life because of justification, as is stated in Romans 8:10: "But if Christ is in you, your body is dead because of sin, yet your spirit is alive because of righteousness."

Verses 11–14

Therefore encourage one another and build each other up, just as in fact you are doing. Now we ask you, brothers, to respect those who work hard among you, who are over you in the Lord and who admonish you. Hold them in the highest regard in love because of their work. Live in peace with each other. And we urge you, brothers, warn those who are idle, encourage the timid, help the weak, be patient with everyone.

11. Encourage. This is the same word we saw at the end of the previous chapter: **Therefore encourage each other with these words** (4:18). In that verse we translated it as "comfort," as the context demanded, and the same would be appropriate in this passage. At the same time, the word **encourage** includes the words "comfort" and "exhort." The apostle, therefore, was telling them to pass on to one another what they had received from the Lord. He added that they should **build each other up**—that is, strengthen each other in the teaching he'd given them. But in case it might appear he was telling them off for being careless, he said at the same time that they were already choosing to do this. We are slow to do what is good, and even those who are most disposed to do it still need to be stimulated.

12. Now we ask you, brothers. Here we come to a very necessary warning. The kingdom of God is often thought of too superficially or at least is not honored as it should be, and godly teachers of the Christian faith are held in contempt. Most of them **admonish** believers about this ingratitude not so much because they see themselves as being despised but because they infer from this that honor is not being given to their Lord. So it is not so much for the advantage of ministers as of the whole church that those who faithfully preside over it should be held in high esteem. And it is for this reason that Paul is so careful to recommend them. To **respect** means here to have regard for or to acknowledge. But Paul intimates that the reason for less honor being shown to teachers themselves than is justly deserved is because their labor is not taken into account.

We must observe, however, what titles of distinction the apostle gives to these pastors. In the first place, he says they **work hard**. From this it follows that all idle people are excluded from the rank of true pastors. Further, he indicated what kind of hard work they were engaged in when he added, **who admonish you** or instruct you. Any people who do not carry out this aspect of their work are not true pastors, even if they glory in the name of *pastor.*

Paul wants leaders to devote themselves to teaching and to preside with no other end in view than that of serving the church and so to be held in no ordinary esteem. The apostle says literally, "Let them be more than abundantly honored," and with good reason, for we must observe the reason he immediately adds—because they **work hard among you.** This **work** is for the building up of the church, the everlasting salvation of souls, the restoration of the world—in short, the kingdom of God and Christ. The excellence and dignity of this work are inestimable. Hence those whom God makes ministers in connection with so great a matter ought to be held in great esteem by us. We may, however, infer from Paul's words that judgment is committed to the church, so that it may distinguish true and faithful pastors from unfaithful pastors. There would have been no reason to make these remarks if the apostle did not mean they should be put into practice by believers. And while he commands that honor should be given to those who **work hard** and to those who through teaching and admonishing govern correctly and faithfully, he definitely does not bestow any honor on those who are idle and wicked, nor does he single them out as deserving this.

Who are over you in the Lord. This refers to spiritual government. Although kings and magistrates are also appointed by God to preside, since the Lord wants the government of the church to be especially recognized as his, those who govern the church in Christ's name and by Christ's command are spoken of as those **who are over you in the Lord.** We may, nevertheless, infer from this that tyrants who rule in opposition to Christ are very far from the ranks of pastors and prelates. It is beyond dispute that anyone who wishes to join the ranks of the true pastors must show that he presides **in the Lord** and in no other way. This is only carried out when the pastor teaches the pure doctrine as if Christ himself were speaking, so that Christ is Lord and Master.

13. In love. According to the Hebrew idiom, **in** here is equivalent to "by" or "with." I prefer to explain this in the following way: The apostle exhorts us not merely to respect faithful ministers but also to love them. Because the doctrine of the Gospel is lovely, it is right that its ministers should be loved.

Live in peace with each other. While this passage has various readings, I approve the rendering that has been given by an old translator and is followed by Erasmus: "Have or cultivate peace with them." Paul, in my opinion, has in mind that it was necessary to oppose Satan's schemes since he never tires of using every ploy to stir up quarrels, disagreements, or enmities between people and pastor. We see every day that pastors are hated by their churches for some trivial reason or for no reason at all because this desire to cultivate peace that Paul recommends so strongly is not exercised at it should be.

14. Warn those who are idle. It is often insisted that the welfare of our brothers and sisters should be the object of our concern. This is done by teaching, admonishing, correcting, and arousing. But since different people have different dispositions, it is with good reason that the apostle commands believers to use a variety of methods to achieve this end. He therefore states that **those who are idle** should be admonished. This means they should be given a sharp reproof so they may return to the correct path, as there is no other way in which they can be brought back to repentance.

Toward **the timid** a different approach must be used, for they are in need of comfort. **The weak** must also be helped. By **timid**, or fainthearted, the apostle meant those who have a broken spirit. While he commanded that **those who are idle** should be restrained with a degree of sternness, he said that **the weak** should be treated with kindness and that **the timid** should receive consolation. It is pointless to reach out to the obstinate, for nothing will reach them.

The apostle, however, recommended that the Thessalonians should **be patient with everyone.** Severity must be tempered with some degree of leniency, even in dealing with **those who are idle.** This patience contrasts with a feeling of irksomeness, for nothing tires us out more than trying to apply the correct cure to the different diseases our brothers and sisters suffer from. The man who has repeatedly comforted a person who is **timid,** if he is called on to do this yet again, may experience great irritation, which will prevent him from carrying out his duty. If by admonishing or reproving we do not immediately see the good that is intended, we lose all hope for success in the future. Paul wanted to curb such impatience by recommending that they **be patient with everyone.**

Verses 15-22

Make sure that nobody pays back wrong for wrong, but always try to be kind to each other and to everyone else. Be joyful always; pray continually; give thanks in all circumstances, for this is God's will for you in Christ Jesus. Do not put out the Spirit's fire; do not treat prophecies with contempt. Test everything. Hold on to the good. Avoid every kind of evil.

15. Make sure that nobody pays back wrong for wrong. Because it is difficult to observe this precept, as we are so inclined to take revenge, the apostle tells us to take care and be on our guard. The words **make sure** denote special care. While the apostle simply forbids us to inflict injuries on each other, there is no doubt that he is also speaking against even the *inclination* to harm somebody else. If we are not to pay back **wrong for wrong**, then every desire for revenge is also wrong. This teaching—not to retaliate after being hurt but to suffer patiently—is unique to Christians. And in case the Thessalonians should think revenge is forbidden only toward their Christian brothers and sisters, the apostle specifically declared that they were to do evil to no one. Many might protest, "Why should it be unlawful for me to take revenge on somebody who is worthless, wicked, and cruel?" But as revenge is forbidden in every case, with no exceptions allowed, we must refrain from ever hurting people.

But always try to be kind to each other. In this last clause the apostle teaches that we must not merely refrain from taking revenge on anyone who has harmed us, but we must cultivate a kind spirit toward **everyone**. Although he intends that it should, in the first instance, be carried out among believers, he later extends this to include **everyone**, no matter how undeserving they may be. We are to make it our aim to follow Paul's command, "Do not be overcome by evil, but overcome evil with good" (Romans 12:21). So the first step toward being **patient** (verse 14) is not to take revenge on anyone. The second step is to bestow favors, even to our enemies.

16. Be joyful always. I think this means keeping calm in adversity. I link these three things—to **be joyful always**, to **pray continually** (verse 17), and to **give thanks in all circumstances** (verse 18). When the apostle recommends constant prayer, he points out the way of rejoicing all the time, for by this means we ask God to alleviate all our troubles. In a similar way Paul also said, "Rejoice in the Lord always. I will say it again: Rejoice!" (Philippians 4:4). He then went on to say, "Let your gentleness be evident to all. The Lord is near" (Philippians 4:5). After this he pointed out the way in which this is to be achieved: "Do not be anxious about anything, but in everything, by prayer and petition, with thanksgiving, present your requests to God" (Philippians 4:6). In that passage we see the source of calm joy and a composed mind that is not unduly disturbed by injuries or adversities. But in case we should be overcome by grief, sorrow, anxiety, and fear, the apostle tells us to rest in God's providential care. And since doubts about whether God cares for us often intrude, he also prescribes the remedy—by prayer we place our anxieties on God's heart, as David also commanded us: "Commit your way to the LORD; trust in him and he will do this" (Psalm 37:5). Peter also speaks of this: "Cast all your anxiety on him [God] because he cares for you" (1 Peter 5:7). Because we find it so difficult to curb our desires, the apostle imposes a curb on them—when we desire what we need, we must at the same time not stop giving thanks to God.

The apostle observes here, almost in the same order, though in fewer words, what he wrote elsewhere. In the first place he wants us to hold God's blessings in high esteem, so that we see them and meditate on them and so overcome all sorrow. Unquestionably, if we consider what Christ has conferred on us, there will be no grief that is so intense that it cannot be alleviated and give way to spiritual joy. If this joy does not reign in us, we are far away from God's kingdom. A godly person acts in a most ungrateful way if he does not so view Christ's righteousness and the hope of eternal life that he can rejoice in the middle of his sorrow.

As, however, our minds are so easily depressed, so that they give in to impatience, we must follow the advice the apostle gives next. Upon being cast down or laid low we can be lifted up again by prayer as we transfer our burdens to God. As, however, there are every day, if not every moment, many things that may disturb our peace and mar our joy, the apostle tells us to **pray continually**. The apostle also says, **Give thanks in all circumstances**. Now, **give thanks** is added for a specific purpose. Many people pray in such a way that they grumble against God and become upset if they do not immediately receive what they have prayed for. But it is better if our desires are not immediately granted and we are content with what God has given us. We will do this if we always give thanks to God when we pray. We may rightly, it is true, ask, even sigh and plead with God; but it must be in such a way that God's will is more acceptable to us than our own.

18. For this is God's will for you. According to Chrysostom, this is linked with **give thanks**. But my opinion is that this phrase has a wider application—God has such a disposition toward us in Christ that even in our afflictions we have good reason to give thanks. What can pacify us better than learning that God embraces us in Christ so tenderly that he turns to our advantage and welfare everything that happens to us? Let us, therefore, bear in mind this special remedy for correcting our impatience—to turn our eyes from looking at evils around us and to direct our gaze in a different direction—to see how God views us in Christ.

19. Do not put out [quench, KJV] **the Spirit's fire.** This metaphor is taken from the power and nature of the Spirit. It is the Spirit's work to illumine our understanding, and it is therefore called our light; it is likewise right to say that we quench him and **put out** his **fire** when we make his grace to be without fruit. Some people think the next verse says the same as this one. Hence, to them, **do not put out the Spirit's fire** is exactly the same as **do not treat prophecies with contempt**. But because the Spirit is quenched in different ways, I make a distinction between these two things. The first is a general statement, while the second is a specific one.

Although treating prophecies with contempt is a way of putting out the Spirit's fire, people are also guilty of quenching the Spirit when, instead of fanning the flames of their spiritual life more and more as they should, they make God's gifts void through neglect. This warning not to quench the Spirit therefore has a wider application than just despising prophecy. **Do not put out the Spirit's fire** means "be enlightened by the Spirit of God, and see that you do not lose that light through your ingratitude." This is an exceedingly useful admonition. We see that those who have "shared in the Holy Spirit" (Hebrews 6:4), when they reject such a precious gift from God or allow themselves to be swept along with the vanity of this world, are struck down blind, so they will be an example to others. Therefore, we must be on our guard against laziness, by which God's light is choked in us.

Those, however, who infer from this that it is in our power either to quench or to cherish the light that is given to us, detract from the efficacy of grace and extol the powers of free will; this is reasoning on false grounds. God works efficaciously in his elect. He does not merely present the light to them but makes them see, opens the eyes of their heart, and keeps them open. But as the flesh is always inclined to indolence, it needs to be stirred by exhortations. What God commands through Paul's mouth, he himself accomplishes inwardly. At the same time, it is our duty to ask the Lord to give us oil for the lamps he has already lighted, that he may keep the wicks pure and may even increase their light.

20. Do not treat prophecies with contempt. This sentence follows on from the previous one. As the Spirit of God illuminates us mainly through doctrine, those who do not give teaching its proper place quench the Spirit as far as they can. We must always remember how God communicates with us. All who want to make progress under the Holy Spirit's direction should allow themselves to be taught by the ministry of prophets.

By the term **prophecies**, however, I do not include the gift of foretelling the future. "Everyone who prophesies speaks to men for their strengthening, encouragement and comfort" (1 Corinthians 14:3). **Prophecies** means the art of interpreting Scripture; a prophet is an interpreter of the will of God. In 1 Corinthians Paul shows that prophetic teaching is for edification, exhortation, and consolation. "He who speaks in a tongue edifies himself, but he who prophesies edifies the church. I would like every one of you to speak in tongues, but I would rather have you prophesy. He who prophesies is greater than one who speaks in tongues, unless he interprets, so that the church may be edified" (1 Corinthians 14:4-5). So prophecy in 1 Thessalonians 5:20 means the interpretation of Scripture properly applied to the people present. Paul forbids us from viewing **prophecies with contempt,** so that we will not wander off into the darkness.

This remarkable statement commends preaching. Fanatics imagine that people who spend their time reading the Scriptures or hearing the Word preached are wasting their time, as if nobody is spiritual without despising Christian teaching. In their pride such people despise the preacher's ministry and even despise Scripture itself as they pretend to be seeking God's Spirit. In addition to this, whatever Satan whispers in their ears, they have the presumption to declare as if it were a secret revelation from the Spirit. Such people are libertines. The more ignorant a person is, the more puffed up he becomes as he swells with his own arrogance. Let us, however, learn from Paul's example to link the Spirit with the human voice, which becomes his instrument.

21. Test everything. As rash people and deceiving spirits often pass off their trifles under the name of prophecy, prophecy itself may be treated with suspicion and even become distasteful. In the same way many people today are put off by the word *preaching*, for many foolish and ignorant people babble worthless words from the pulpit. Such people bring prophecy into disrepute. So Paul exhorted the Thessalonians to **test everything**, meaning by this that as everyone will not speak with God's Spirit in him, we must judge everything we hear before any teaching is condemned or accepted.

There are two pitfalls to avoid here. Some people reject every kind of Christian teaching indiscriminately because they have been previously deceived by a false prophet. Other people welcome uncritically every word they hear that is spoken in God's name. Both groups have a faulty understanding. The former have been saturated with prejudice and so are unable to make any progress. The latter rashly expose themselves to "every wind of teaching" (Ephesians 4:14). Paul advised the Thessalonians to steer a middle course between these two extremes. He forbade them from condemning anything without first examining it. He also told them to exercise judgment before receiving any teaching as being true. Unquestionably, we should respect prophecy that is said to have come from God. But just as examination or discrimination should take place before anything is rejected, so it must also precede the welcoming of true and sound doctrine. It is not right that godly people should indiscriminately accept either false teaching or true teaching. From this we infer that believers have the spirit of discernment given to them by God, so that they may reject the false teachings of impostors. If they were not endowed with this gift of discrimination, it would be pointless for Paul to tell them, **Test everything. Hold on to the good.** If, however, we feel that we do not have the ability to discern between what is false and what is true, we must seek this ability from the Spirit, who speaks through his prophets. But the Lord declares here, through the writing of Paul, that true Christian teaching should never be absent in any church as a result of the ignorance or abuse of men. Since the abolition of prophecy ruins the church, let us allow heaven and earth to mingle rather than allow prophecy to cease.

Paul, however, may appear here to give too much freedom in teaching when he says, **test everything**. For before we can test anything, we must first of all listen to it. This opens the door to impostors who peddle their false teaching. I answer that in this instance he did not at all require that such false teachers should be given a hearing. Elsewhere Paul taught that the mouths of false teachers must be closed. "For there are many rebellious people, mere talkers and deceivers, especially those of the circumcision group. They must be silenced, because they are ruining whole households by teaching things they ought not to teach—and that for the sake of dishonest gain" (Titus 1:10-11). While Paul insists that false teachers must not be listened to, he also highly commends those who have been called to teach the Christian faith. "Now the overseer must be . . . able to teach" (1 Timothy 3:2).

22. Avoid every kind of evil. Some people believe this is a universal statement, as if Paul were commanding the Thessalonians to abstain from everything that might even have the appearance of evil. If that were the case, the meaning would be that it is not enough to have the inner witness of conscience unless at the same time attention is given to Christian brothers and sisters, so that no offense is ever given.

Those who interpret **kind** as if it were a subdivision of a general term fall into serious error. The apostle has used the word **kind** to mean what we commonly call "appearance." It may also be translated as either "evil appearance" or "appearance of evil." The meaning, however, is the same. I prefer Chrysostom's and Ambrose's interpretation, as they link this sentence with the previous one. At the same time, neither of them explains Paul's meaning and perhaps have not really hit on what he intends. I shall briefly state my view.

In the first place, the phrase "appearance of evil" or "evil appearance," I think, means false teaching that has not yet been exposed can on good grounds be rejected. At the same time a lurking suspicion is left in the mind, and a nasty taste is left in the mouth in case any poison should be present. Therefore Paul commands that we should abstain from the kind of teaching that has an appearance of being evil, although it is not really evil. He does this so that it is not completely rejected and at the same time so that it should not be received. Why did he previously say, **Test everything. Hold on to the good** (verse 21), while he now says that we should **avoid every kind of evil**? He says this because when truth has been brought to light through careful examination, it is definitely right in that case to give it credit. But if there is any suspicion that the teaching is false, or if the mind has its doubts about the teaching, it is correct in such cases to step back and suspend our judgment so that we do not accept anything with a doubtful or troubled conscience. In short, he shows us in what way prophecy will be useful to us, without it becoming a danger. If we take pains to **test everything**, we will be free from levity and from accepting anything too speedily.

Verses 23-28

May God himself, the God of peace, sanctify you through and through. May your whole spirit, soul and body be kept blameless at the coming of our Lord Jesus Christ. The one who calls you is faithful and he will do it. Brothers, pray for us. Greet all the brothers with a holy kiss. I charge you before the Lord to have this letter read to all the brothers. The grace of our Lord Jesus Christ be with you.

23. Having given various injunctions, the apostle now moves on to prayer. Unquestionably, teaching will be of no benefit to us unless God plants it in our minds. From this we see how badly people behave who do not measure the strength of man by God's precepts. So Paul, who knew that all teaching is useless unless God engraves it on our hearts, pleaded with God to **sanctify** the Thessalonians. I do not fully understand why Paul calls God **the God of peace** here, though this may refer to what had been said in earlier verses, where Paul mentioned brotherly agreement, patience, and equanimity.

We know, however, that the term **sanctify** includes the whole renewal of a person. The Thessalonians, it is true, had been partly renewed, but Paul wanted them to be completely renewed. From this we infer that we must throughout all of our lives make progress in the pursuit of holiness. But if it is God's role to renew the whole person, then free will has no part to play in this. For if it had been our task to cooperate with God, Paul would have said, "May God help or promote your sanctification." But when he said, **May God himself . . . sanctify you**, Paul made God the sole Author of the complete work.

May your whole spirit . . . This was added as an explanation, so that we would know what the sanctification of the whole person is, when he is kept entirely pure and unpolluted in **spirit, soul and body** until the day of Christ. But because this perfection is never attained in this life, it is fitting that some progress in purity should be made each day, and some pollution cleared away daily, so long as we live in this world.

We must notice, however, the divisions of the constituent parts of a man. Sometimes a man is said to consist simply of **body** and **soul**, and in that instance the **soul** refers to the immortal spirit, which has taken up residence in the body. As the **soul**, however, has two principal faculties—the understanding and the will—the Scripture on some occasions mentions these two things separately, referring to the power and nature of the **soul**.

But in that case the term **soul** is used to mean the center of the affections, the part that is contrasted with the **spirit**. Hence, when we find the word **spirit** mentioned here, we are to understand that it refers to reason or intelligence, while the term **soul** means the will and all the affections.

I am aware that many people explain Paul's words in a different way, for they think that the term *soul* means vital movement and that the term *spirit* means the part of man that has been renewed. But this would make Paul's prayer absurd. Besides, the Scripture uses this term in a different way, as I have said. When Isaiah says, "My soul yearns for you in the night; in the morning my spirit longs for you" (Isaiah 26:9), no one doubts that he is speaking of his understanding and affection, and thus the two parts of the soul are enumerated. These two terms are often linked together in the Psalms, where they have the same meaning. This also is the best way to understand Paul's statement here. How can the whole person be complete except when his thoughts are pure and holy, when all his affections are properly regulated, when, in short, the body itself is only engaged in good deeds? The affections hold a middle place for giving commands, while the body does what it is told. We now see how each part relates to the whole. A man is pure and complete when he does not think anything in his mind, desires nothing in his heart, and does nothing with his body except what is approved of by God. As, however, Paul in this way commits to God the keeping of the whole man and all his parts, we must infer from this that we are exposed to countless dangers unless we are protected by divine guardianship.

24. The one who calls you is faithful. The apostle showed by his prayer what great concern he had for the welfare of the Thessalonians, and he now confirmed them in an assurance of divine grace. Observe, however, what argument he used as he promised them the never-failing help of God. God was the one who had called them. By these words Paul means that when the Lord has adopted us as his sons and daughters, we may expect that his grace will always continue and help us. God does not promise to be a Father to us for just one day but adopts us so he can cherish us forever. So our calling should be seen by us as evidence of everlasting grace, for he will not leave the work of his hands unfinished (see Psalm 138:8). Paul, however, addresses believers, who have not been merely called by outward preaching but have been effectively brought by Christ to the Father, so that they would be included in the number of his sons.

26. Greet all the brothers with a holy kiss. As far as the **kiss** is concerned, this was a normal means of greeting. In these words, however, Paul declared his affection to all the saints.

27. I charge you before the Lord. It is not clear if Paul feared that, as often happened, spiteful and envious people would suppress this letter or if he wanted to guard against some other danger—perhaps that some people on account of ill-advised caution would read it to only a small number of people without showing it to everyone. There will always be some people who say there is no advantage in making things widely known even though they recognize those things are excellent. Satan could contrive many tricks or pretexts in order to keep the letter from being read by everyone, and we deduce from Paul's words how much he opposed this happening. It is no frivolous thing to say, **I charge you before the Lord to have this letter read to all the brothers**. We find, therefore, that God's Spirit wanted those things that he set out in this letter, through Paul's ministry, to be made known throughout the church. There are those even today who prevent the people of God from reading the writings of Paul, being unmoved by this strict command.

2 Thessalonians

Dedication

The author's dedicatory letter to Benedict Textor, Physician.

While you are reckoned to excel in the knowledge of your profession by those who are competent judges in that matter, I, for my part, have always regarded as a very high excellence that strict faithfulness and diligence that you are accustomed to exercise, both in attending the sick and in giving advice. But more especially in either restoring or establishing my own health, I have observed you to be most careful, so that it was easy to perceive that you were influenced not so much by regard to a particular individual as by anxiety and concern for the common welfare of the church. Another, perhaps, might think that the kindness was smaller from its not having been shown simply to himself as an individual; but as for me, I think myself on the contrary to be under a double obligation to you, on the ground that while you omitted nothing whatever in discharging the office of a friend, you were at the same time equally concerned as to my ministry, which ought to be dearer to me than my life. The remembrance, besides, of my departed wife reminds me daily how much I owe you, not only because she was frequently through your assistance raised up and was in one instance restored from a serious and dangerous illness, but that even in that last disease, which took her away from us, you left nothing undone in the way of industry, labor, and effort with a view to helping her. Further, as you do not allow me to give you any other remuneration, I have thought of inscribing your name upon this commentary, in order that there may be some token of my good wishes toward you in return.

John Calvin, Geneva, 1 July, 1550

Argument of the Second Letter to the Thessalonians

It does not appear to me probable that this letter was sent from Rome, as the Greek manuscripts commonly say; for the apostle would have mentioned his chains, as he does in his other letters written from prison. Besides, near the end of chapter 3 he mentions that he is in danger from unreasonable and wicked men. From this it may be gathered that when he was going to Jerusalem, he wrote this letter in the course of the journey. It was also from an ancient date a very generally accepted opinion among the Latins that it was written from Athens.

The occasion, however, of his writing was this—that the Thessalonians might not reckon themselves overlooked because Paul had not visited them when making a speedy journey to some other place. In the first chapter he tells them to be patient. In the second chapter a vain and groundless fancy, which had gained circulation, about the coming of Christ being at hand is set aside by him in his arguments—there must first come a rebellion in the church, and a great part of the world must abandon following God, and even more, Antichrist must rule in God's temple. In the third chapter, after having commended himself to their prayers and having in a few words encouraged them to persevere, he commands that those who live a life of ease at other peoples' expense should be severely rebuked. If they do not obey these admonitions, they are to be excommunicated.

2 Thessalonians
Chapter 1

Verses 1-7a

Paul, Silas and Timothy, To the church of the Thessalonians in God our Father and the Lord Jesus Christ: Grace and peace to you from God the Father and the Lord Jesus Christ. We ought always to thank God for you, brothers, and rightly so, because your faith is growing more and more, and the love every one of you has for each other is increasing. Therefore, among God's churches we boast about your perseverance and faith in all the persecutions and trials you are enduring. All this is evidence that God's judgment is right, and as a result you will be counted worthy of the kingdom of God, for which you are suffering. God is just: He will pay back trouble to those who trouble you and give relief to you who are troubled, and to us as well.

1. To the church of the Thessalonians in God our Father and the Lord Jesus Christ. This salutation means that the Thessalonians had not merely been gathered together under the banner of faith, in order to worship one God the Father and to confide in Christ, but were the work and building of both the Father and of Christ. God adopts us for himself and regenerates us, and we are in Christ because of the Father. "It is because of him [God] that you are in Christ Jesus, who has become for us wisdom from God—that is, our righteousness, holiness and redemption" (1 Corinthians 1:30).

3. We ought always to thank God for you. The apostle begins by commending the Thessalonians so he could have the opportunity to pass on an exhortation to them. Using such an approach we will have more success among those who have already started the course. Their previous progress is not passed over in silence, but we can remind them how much farther they still have to travel and urge them to make progress. The apostle had in his previous letter commended their faith and love, and he now declares that they were increasing in both of these: **because your faith is growing more and more, and the love every one of you has for each other is increasing.** Unquestionably, this course of action should be followed by all godly people—to examine themselves every day and see how far they have progressed. This, therefore, is the true commendation of believers—their **growing** daily in **faith** and **love.**

When the apostle says **always,** he means he is constantly given new reasons to give thanks for them. Paul had previously given thanks to God on their account and had further reasons to do so again because of the progress they made each day. When, however, he gave thanks to God on their account, he declared that their new progress, no less than their initial progress, in faith and love were from God, for if they made progress from the strength of men, Paul's thanksgiving to God would be false or at least worthless. Further, the apostle showed that the advances they made were not superficial or even ordinary but most abundant. So our slowness in making progress is even more disgraceful, inasmuch as we scarcely advance by one foot over a long period of time.

And rightly so. In these words Paul shows that we are bound to give thanks to God not only when he does us good, but also when we take into account the favors bestowed by him on our brethren. Wherever the goodness of God shines, we should extol it. Further, the well-being of our brethren should be so dear to us that we should apply to ourselves everything that has been conferred on them. More than that, if we consider the nature and sacredness of the unity of Christ's Body, such a mutual fellowship will exist among us that we will reckon the benefits conferred on an individual member as a benefit for the whole church. So by extolling God's benefits, we must always have in mind the whole body of the church.

4. The apostle could not have bestowed higher commendation on them than by saying that he used them as examples for other churches to follow—**among God's churches we boast about your perseverance and faith.** Paul did not boast about the faith of the Thessalonians from a spirit of ambition, but inasmuch as his commendation of them might be a spur to make other Christians imitate them. Paul did not say, however, that he gloried in their faith and love, but in their **perseverance and faith.** Here **perseverance** is the fruit and proof of **faith.** "We glory in the perseverance that springs from faith, and we bear witness that it eminently shines out from you." Unquestionably, nothing sustains us in trials as much as faith does, for we know how we begin to sink as soon as God's promises leave us. Hence the more we advance in faith, the more we are endued with perseverance to endure everything with fortitude. Weakness and impatience are signs of unbelief on our part. The effect of faith is especially apparent when persecutions are endured for the sake of the Gospel.

5. All this is evidence that God's judgment is right. However other people may interpret these words, I think their true meaning is as follows: The injuries and persecutions that innocent and godly people endure from the wicked clearly show that God will one day be the Judge of the world. This statement differs completely from the profane idea we hear all the time whenever it goes badly with the good and well for the wicked. We think the world is run by mere chance, and we leave God out of our thinking. In this way ungodly and contemptuous thoughts grip people's hearts, as Solomon said: "This is the evil in everything that happens under the sun: The same destiny overtakes all. The hearts of men, moreover, are full of evil and there is madness in their hearts while they live" (Ecclesiastes 9:3). People who go through undeserved suffering either blame God or think he is unconcerned with their plight. This is how Ovid spoke about this: "When misfortunes overtake the good, I am tempted to think that there are no gods." In addition to this Asaph confessed that because he saw that the world was in such a state of confusion, he almost lost his footing, as if he were on a slippery path.

> *Surely God is good to Israel, to those who are pure in heart. But as for me, my feet had almost slipped; I had nearly lost my foothold. For I envied the arrogant when I saw the prosperity of the wicked. They have no struggles; their bodies are healthy and strong. They are free from the burdens common to man; they are not plagued by human ills. Therefore pride is their necklace; they clothe themselves with violence. From their callous hearts comes iniquity; the evil conceits of their minds know no limits. They scoff, and speak with malice; in their arrogance they threaten oppression. Their mouths lay claim to heaven, and their tongues take possession of the earth. Therefore their people turn to them and drink up waters in abundance. They say, "How can God know? Does the Most High have knowledge?" This is what the wicked are like—always carefree, they increase in wealth.*
> —Psalm 73:1-12

On the other hand, the wicked become more insolent the more prosperous they become, as if their crimes will never be punished. They are just like Dionysius the tyrant, who after he had plundered the temple went off on a sea voyage, boasting that the gods had given him a favorable wind. In short, when we see that the cruelty of the wicked against the innocent seems to go unpunished, earthly thinking concludes that God does not judge people and that evil people escape any kind of punishment, while there is no reward for the righteous. Paul, however, declared that in God's sparing the wicked for a time and overlooking the wounds inflicted on his people, his coming judgment is shown to us. Paul takes it for granted that God, since he is a just Judge, will one day restore peace to the afflicted, who are now unjustly persecuted, and will repay the oppressors of godly people with the punishment they deserve.

If we hang on to this principle of faith, that God is the just Judge of the world and that it is his office to pay back to everyone according to their deeds, a second principle is bound to follow: The present disorderly state of affairs is a demonstration of the judgment that is yet to come. If God is the righteous Judge of the world, those things that are now confused must of necessity be restored to an orderly state. At present nothing is more disorderly than that the wicked with impunity molest the good and swagger around with unbridled violence, while the good are cruelly harassed without any fault on their part. From this it may be correctly inferred that God will one day ascend the judgment seat and will remedy the state of affairs in this world and put them right.

Hence Paul's statement that **all this is evidence that God's judgment is right** is the basis of the doctrine that God demonstrates a coming judgment when he refrains for the present from exercising the office of judge. And, unquestionably, if matters were all orderly now, so that it was clear that God's judgment had already taken place, we might always long to stay on this earth. God, in order to stir up the hope of a coming judgment, does for the present only to a certain extent judge the world. He gives us, it is true, many tokens of his judgment, but in a way that makes us hope for a future judgment. This is a remarkable passage in Paul's writing, as it teaches us how our minds should always be elevated above all worldly events whenever we suffer any adversity, so the righteous judgment of God will be at the forefront of our minds, which will raise us above this world.

You will be counted worthy. No persecutions can make us **worthy of the kingdom of God,** nor does Paul here argue about the basis for being worthy of God's kingdom. He is simply applying the normal teaching of Scripture—that God destroys in us the things of the world, that he may replace them with a better life. In addition to this, God shows us the value of eternal life through our afflictions. In short, Paul simply points out the way in which believers are prepared and, as it were, polished under God's anvil, inasmuch as through afflictions they are taught to renounce the world and aim for God's heavenly kingdom. Further, they are strengthened in the hope of eternal life as they fight for Christ. This is the entrance Christ taught his disciples about: "Enter through the narrow gate. For wide is the gate and broad is the road that leads to destruction, and many enter through it" (Matthew 7:13). "Make every effort to enter through the narrow door, because many, I tell you, will try to enter and will not be able to" (Luke 13:24).

6. God is just: He will pay back trouble to those who trouble you. We have already said why Paul mentioned God's vengeance on the wicked—

that we may learn to rest in the expectation of a judgment to come, though it is also necessary that they should be punished for their crimes. Believers, however, at the same time understand from this that there is no reason why they should envy the momentary and passing happiness of the wicked, which will before long be replaced by dreadful destruction. Paul's statement that God will **give relief** (verse 7) to the Thessalonians is in line with Acts 3:19, which calls the day of the last judgment "times of refreshing."

7. Paul now adds **and to us as well** in order to give credence to his teaching from his own personal experience. He demonstrates that he was not talking about some vague philosophical idea but was identifying himself with the Thessalonians and their troubles. We know how much more authority is due to those who after lengthy practice have been exercised in those things about which they teach and do not require from others anything they themselves are not prepared to do. Paul, therefore, did not remain in the shade, giving instructions to the Thessalonians about how they should fight in the heat of the sun; rather, fighting vigorously, he exhorted them to join in the same battle.

Verses 7b-10

This will happen when the Lord Jesus is revealed from heaven in blazing fire with his powerful angels. He will punish those who do not know God and do not obey the gospel of our Lord Jesus. They will be punished with everlasting destruction and shut out from the presence of the Lord and from the majesty of his power on the day he comes to be glorified in his holy people and to be marveled at among all those who have believed. This includes you, because you believed our testimony to you.

7b. When the Lord Jesus is revealed from heaven. We have here a confirmation of the previous statement. Since it is one of the articles of our faith that Christ will come from heaven and that his coming will not be in vain, faith should seek out the purpose of his coming—that he may come as a Redeemer to his own people and, more than that, judge the whole world. The following description has this end in sight, so that the godly may understand God is concerned about their troubles and will definitely bring dreadful judgment on his enemies. The main reason for our grief and distress is that we think God is unmoved by our calamities. David from time to time expresses this in his psalms, being consumed with the pride and insolence of his enemies. Hence Paul's teaching here, given for the comfort of believers. At the same time he depicts the judgment of Christ as a time of horror and terror, so that the Thessalonians may not be disheartened by their present oppressed state as they see themselves trampled on by the wicked.

The Lord Jesus is revealed from heaven in blazing fire. The nature of this **fire**, and what materials are used, I leave to those people who are full of idle curiosity. I am content to hold on to the main point of Paul's teaching—Christ will be a most strict avenger of the wounds that the wicked inflict on us. The metaphor, however, of *blazing* fire is very common in Scripture when God's anger is mentioned.

By **his powerful angels**, Paul means those in whom he will exercise his power; Christ will bring the angels with him in order to display the glory of his kingdom.

8. He will punish those who do not know God. In order to fully convince the believers that the persecutions they endure at present will not go unpunished in the future, the apostle teaches that this involves the interests of God himself, inasmuch as the same people who persecute the godly are guilty of rebellion against God. So it is necessary that God should inflict vengeance on them, not merely with a view to our salvation, but also for the sake of his own glory. Furthermore, this expression, **he will punish**, relates to Christ, for Paul intimates that this office is assigned to Christ by God the Father. Some may ask whether it is right for us to desire vengeance, for Paul promises it as if it is correct to want it. I answer that it is not right to want vengeance on people in general, for we are commanded to wish them well. Besides, although we may in a general way desire vengeance on the wicked, yet, as we are not yet able to determine who they are, we should seek everyone's welfare. In the meantime, the ruin of the wicked may be rightly looked forward to, provided our hearts are pure and controlled by zeal for God and there is no feeling of inordinate desire.

The apostle identifies unbelievers in two ways: They **do not know God**, and they **do not obey the gospel of our Lord Jesus**. If the Gospel is not obeyed through faith, as Paul teaches in the first and last chapters of his letter to the Romans, unbelief will take over. Paul also accuses those who do not believe in God of being ignorant about God, for a living acquaintance with God will itself produce reverence toward him. So unbelief is always blind, not as if unbelievers were completely devoid of light and intelligence, but because they have their understanding darkened in such a way that "though seeing, they do not see; though hearing, they do not hear or understand" (Matthew 13:13). It is not without good reason that Christ declares that "this is eternal life: that they may know you, the only true God" (John 17:3). So from lack of this salutary knowledge follows contempt for God and, in short, death.

9. They will be punished with everlasting destruction and shut out from the presence of the Lord. The apostle shows, by way of contrast, the nature of the punishment he is talking about—destruction without end and an undying death. The perpetuity of death is shown because it is set against the glory of Christ, which is eternal and has no end. Accordingly, the effect of that death will never end. From this the dreadful severity of the punishment is inferred, inasmuch as it will be in proportion to the glory and majesty of Christ.

10. On the day he comes to be glorified in his holy people. As Paul had just written about the punishment of the wicked, so he now returns to the godly and says that Christ will come so that he may **be glorified** in them. This means that he will irradiate them with his glory and that they will take part in this. Christ will not have this glory for himself alone, but it will possess all the saints. The crowning and choice consolation of the godly will be that when the Son of God is manifested in the glory of his kingdom, he will gather them into the same fellowship with himself. There is an implied contrast between the present condition in which believers labor and groan and that final restoration. They are *now* exposed to the reproaches of the world and are looked on as being vile and worthless; but *then* they will be precious and full of dignity, for Christ will pour his glory upon them. The purpose of this teaching is so the godly may pursue their brief earthly journey as their minds are set on the future manifestation of Christ's kingdom. Paul mentioned Christ's coming in power so that the Thessalonians could in hope leap forward to that blessed resurrection that still remains hidden.

Notice, too, that after Paul uses the expression **holy people** he adds, by way of explanation, **among all those who have believed.** By this he means that there is no holiness in anyone if they do not have faith. In fact, people without faith are all ungodly. In this verse he also says, **on the day,** so that he could curb the desire of the believers in case they were overcome in their eagerness about the Lord's coming.

You believed our testimony to you. What the apostle had said in a general way to saints, he now applied to the Thessalonians, so they might not doubt that they were included with God's holy people. "Because," he said, "my preaching has been accepted among you, Christ has already enrolled you in the number of his own people, whom he will make partakers of his glory." He calls his doctrine a **testimony** because the apostles were Christ's witnesses. "But you will receive power when the Holy Spirit comes on you; and you will be my witnesses in Jerusalem, and in all Judea and Samaria, and to the ends of the earth" (Acts 1:8). God's promises are ratified in us when they gain credit with us.

Verses 11-12

With this in mind, we constantly pray for you, that our God may count you worthy of his calling, and that by his power he may fulfill

every good purpose of yours and every act prompted by your faith. We pray this so that the name of our Lord Jesus may be glorified in you, and you in him, according to the grace of our God and the Lord Jesus Christ.

11. With this in mind, we constantly pray for you. Paul declared that he prayed for the Thessalonians in order to show that they were continually in need of God's help. When the apostle said, **with this in mind**, he meant, in order that they might reach the final goal. This is clear from the following words: **that God may . . . fulfill every good purpose of yours.** It may seem, however, as if what the apostle mentioned first of all was unnecessary, for God had already counted them **worthy of his calling.** Paul spoke, however, about the end or completion, which depends on perseverance.

He may fulfill. Paul moved on to an amazing height in extolling God's grace, for he did not content himself with the term **every good purpose**, which amounts to the same thing—grace. When we are instructed that God's gracious purpose is the cause of our salvation, and that it has the goodness of the same God as its foundation, are we not more than mad if we attempt to ascribe anything, no matter how small it is, to our own merits? These words are particularly emphatic. He might have said, "that your faith may be fulfilled," but he said instead that it is God's **good purpose.** Furthermore, he expressed the idea even more clearly by saying that God was prompted by nothing but his own goodness, for he finds nothing in us but misery.

Paul does not ascribe to God's grace merely the beginning of our salvation but every part of it. So the arguments of the Sophists that we are indeed anticipated by God's grace but subsequently are helped through our own merits can be set aside. Paul recognizes in the whole progress of our salvation nothing but the pure grace of God. As, however, the **good purpose** of God has already been accomplished in him, Paul explains this by saying that this is a work of **faith.** While Paul calls this an **act**, he ascribes even this to God. It is as if he had said, "that he may complete the building of faith he has begun."

It is also not without good reason that Paul says, **by his power**, for he intimates that the perfecting of faith is an arduous matter and one of greatest difficulty. This also we know only too well from experience, if we consider how great our weakness is, how many hindrances obstruct us on every side and how severe the attacks of Satan are. Hence, unless the power of God helps us in a special way, faith will never rise to its full height.

12. That the name of our Lord Jesus may be glorified in you. The apostle now calls us back to the main purpose of our lives—that we may promote the Lord's glory. What he adds, however, is particularly worth noting—those who have advanced the glory of Christ will also in their turn be glorified in him. In this, first of all, the wonderful goodness of God shines out—he will have his glory brightly revealed in us who are at present covered with ignominy. It is a double miracle—he who afterwards irradiates us with his glory will do the same to us in return. It is solely by the guidance of the Holy Spirit that our life is made to contribute to God's glory; and thus fruit arising from this must be ascribed to the great mercy of God. In the meantime, we must aim with all our might to promote Christ's glory, which is linked to ours.

2 Thessalonians
Chapter 2

Verses 1-2

Concerning the coming of our Lord Jesus Christ and our being gathered to him, we ask you, brothers, not to become easily unsettled or alarmed by some prophecy, report or letter supposed to have come from us, saying that the day of the Lord has already come.

1. **Concerning the coming of our Lord Jesus Christ.** This may indeed be translated, *concerning* the coming, but it is better to read it as an earnest entreaty, taken from the subject in hand. Paul solemnly commanded the Thessalonian believers by the coming of Christ not to imagine rashly that the Lord's day was at hand, and he at the same time admonished us not to think of it except with reverence and sobriety, for it is customary to draw aside on the basis of those things that are regarded by us with reverence. The meaning therefore is, "As you set a high value on the coming of Christ, when he will gather us to himself and will truly perfect that unity of the body that we cherish as yet only in part through faith, so I earnestly beseech you by his coming not to be too credulous should anyone affirm, on whatever pretext, that his day is at hand."

As Paul had in his former letter alluded to some extent to the resurrection, it is possible that some fickle and fanatical people used this occasion to make a prediction about an imminent coming of Christ. It is unlikely that this error had taken hold previously among the Thessalonians, for Timothy, on his return there, had informed Paul about their condition, and as a prudent and experienced man had left out nothing of importance. Thus I am of the opinion that when Paul's letter had been read, which contained a living argument about the resurrection, some people indulged their curiosity and guessed when this would take place. This, however, was a fancy that was singularly destructive and utterly ruinous, as were other things of the same nature that were later disseminated with the help of the wily Satan. When any day is said to be near, if it does not arrive quickly, people are naturally impatient about the long delay, their spirits begin to languish, and that languishing soon turns into despair.

This, therefore, was Satan's subtle trick. Since he could not openly demolish the hope of a resurrection in order to secretly undermine that future event, he promised falsely that it would soon arrive. Afterwards, too, he did not cease to contrive various things with the intent of effacing, little by little, the belief of a resurrection from people's minds, since he could not openly eradicate it. It is indeed a believable thing to say that the day of our redemption is definitely fixed, and on this account it is welcomed with open arms by people in general, just as we see that the dreams of Lactantius and the followers of Celsus of old gave much delight, and yet they had no motive except to overthrow the hope of a resurrection. This was not the design of Lactantius alone but of Satan, in line with his deceiving nature and his perverted curiosity. People who follow Satan leave nothing definite or fixed in religion, and even to the present day he does not cease to use these same tactics. We now see how necessary Paul's admonition was. But for this all religion would have been overturned among the Thessalonians under a specious pretext.

2. Paul pointed out that there were three types of imposture they needed to be on guard against—**prophecy, report or letter supposed to have come from us**—that is, a spurious letter. By the term **prophecy** Paul meant false prophesies, and it appears that this way of speaking was common among the godly, so that they gave it the name of **prophecy** in order to make it honorable. In order for prophecies to have due authority, we must look to God's Spirit and not to men. But since the devil often "masquerades as an angel of light" (2 Corinthians 11:14), impostors stole the title of **prophecy** in order to fool the simpleminded. Even though Paul could have unmasked them, he preferred to speak in this way, by way of concession, as if he said, "However they may pretend to have the spirit of revelation, do not believe them." John says a similar thing: "Dear friends, do not believe every spirit, but test the spirits to see whether they are from God, because many false prophets have gone out into the world" (1 John 4:1).

Report, in my opinion, includes every kind of teaching; false teachers insist on using false reason, conjecture, and pretexts. Paul added, **or letter supposed to have come from us**, evidence that this impudence has a long history—that of using the names of great people. God's grace toward us is the more wonderful in that while Paul's name was used in spurious writings, his writings have nevertheless been preserved even to our times. This could not have taken place accidentally or as the effect of mere human industry if God himself had not by his power restrained Satan and all his ministers.

Saying that the day of the Lord has already come. This may seem to contradict many passages of Scripture, where the Spirit declares that day to be at hand. But the solution is easy, for it is at hand with regard to God, with whom one day is as a thousand years (see 2 Peter 3:8). In the meantime, the Lord wants us to constantly wait for him in such a way that we do not limit him to a certain time. "Therefore keep watch, because you do not know on what day your Lord will come" (Matthew 24:42). On the other hand, those false prophets whom Paul exposed should not have kept men's minds in suspense, telling them to be assured about his speedy coming, so that their hearers would not become disillusioned by the great delay.

Verses 3-4

Don't let anyone deceive you in any way, for that day will not come until the rebellion occurs and the man of lawlessness is revealed, the man doomed to destruction. He opposes and exalts himself over everything that is called God or is worshiped, so that he even sets himself up in God's temple, proclaiming himself to be God.

3. Don't let anyone deceive you. Paul gave the Thessalonians a melancholy prediction about the future scattering of the church, so they would not make empty promises to themselves about the imminent arrival of the joyful day of redemption. This discourse corresponds with the one Christ gave in the presence of his disciples when they asked him questions about the end of the world. He exhorted them to prepare themselves to endure hard conflicts.

Jesus left the temple and was walking away when his disciples came up to him to call his attention to its buildings. "Do you see all these things?" he asked. "I tell you the truth, not one stone here will be left on another; every one will be thrown down." As Jesus was sitting on the Mount of Olives, the disciples came to him privately. "Tell us," they said, "when will this happen, and what will be the sign of your coming and of the end of the age?" Jesus answered: "Watch out that no one deceives you. For many will come in my name, claiming, 'I am the Christ,' and will deceive many. You will hear of wars and rumors of wars, but see to it that you are not alarmed. Such things must happen, but the end is still to come. Nation will rise against nation, and kingdom against kingdom. There will be famines and earthquakes in various places. All these are the beginning of birth pains. Then you will be handed over to be persecuted and put to death, and you will be hated by all nations because of me. At that time many will turn away from the faith and will betray and hate each other, and many false prophets will appear and deceive many people. Because of the increase of wickedness, the love of most will grow cold, but he who stands firm to the end will be saved. And this gospel of the kingdom will be preached in the whole world as a testimony to all nations, and then the end will come. So when you see standing in the holy place 'the abomination that causes desolation,' spoken of through the prophet Daniel—let the reader understand—then let those who are in Judea flee to the mountains. Let no one on the roof of his house go down to take anything out of the house. Let no one in the field go back to get his cloak. How dreadful it will be in those days for pregnant women and nursing mothers! Pray that your flight will not take place in winter or on the Sabbath. For then there will be great distress, unequaled from the beginning of the world until now—and never to be equaled again. If those days had not been cut short, no one would survive, but for the sake of the elect those days will be shortened. At that time if anyone says to you, 'Look, here is the Christ!' or, 'There he is!' do not believe it. For false Christs and false prophets will appear and perform great signs and miracles to deceive even the elect—if that were possible. See, I have told you ahead of time."

—Matthew 24:1-25

In the middle of this Christ says, "the end is still to come" (verse 6), and, "all these are the beginning of birth pains" (verse 8). In the same way, Paul declares that believers must engage in the battle for a long time before they will triumph.

We have here in 1 Thessalonians 2, however, a remarkable passage, one that is worthy of close attention. It was a serious and dangerous temptation, one that might shake even the most resolute followers of Christ and make them lose their footing, to think that the church, which had been raised up gradually though great labors and now stood after facing many difficulties, could fall down suddenly, as if by a storm. So Paul fortified their minds to face such impending dangers. This teaching was not just for the benefit of the Thessalonians but for all godly people, so that when the church was scattered through persecution believers would not be alarmed, as though they were taken by surprise by an unexpected event.

Since commentators have twisted this passage in various ways, we must first of all try to discover Paul's true meaning. He said that the day of Christ will not come until the world has fallen into apostasy and the reign of Antichrist has gained a foothold in the church. The interpretation some have given of this passage, that it refers to the collapse of the Roman Empire, is too ignorant to require a lengthy refutation. I am also surprised that so many writers, in other respects learned, have fallen into error in a matter that is so easy, were it not that when one has made a mistake, countless others follow as a consequence. Paul therefore uses the term **rebellion** or "apostasy" to mean a treacherous departure from God, not on the part of one person or a few individuals, but such as would spread far among a wide circle of people. Now, nobody can be called an apostate but he who had previously professed to follow Christ and the Gospel. Paul, therefore, is predicting a general **rebellion** in the visible church. "The church must be reduced to an unsightly and dreadful state of ruin before its full restoration can take place."

From this it is easy to see how useful Paul's prediction is, for it might have seemed as though the church could not have been God's building if it was suddenly overthrown and lay in ruins for so long, had Paul not a long time ago intimated that this would happen. In addition to this, many people today, when they think about how the church has been scattered by persecution for so long, begin to waver, as if this had not been God's purpose. The weak, however, have something to rest on when they learn that the unseemly state of the church was predicted long ago. We will soon see why the Lord allowed the church, or at least what appeared to be the church, to fall into such a shameful state.

Is revealed. The contrived stories about Nero were no better than an old wives' tale. The story says that Nero was carried up from this world and was destined to return in order to harass the church with his wickedness. [The strange idea referred to here by Calvin appears in Cornelius Lapide's commentary on Revelation 13:3, "One of the heads of the beast seemed to have had a fatal wound, but the fatal wound had been healed," which is said to refer to Nero who, after he had been killed, was supposed to have been raised up, as it were, and to have appeared again in the person of Domitian, his successor. So some commentators thought that Nero would be the Antichrist and would be raised up and appear again at the end of the world. —*Editor's note*] Paul, however, does not speak about an individual but about a kingdom that Satan would take hold of, so that he might set up a seat of abomination in the middle of God's temple—which we see accomplished in Popery. The revolt, it is true, has spread more widely. All heretics have broken the unity of the church by their sects, and thus there have been a corresponding number of rebellions against Christ.

Paul, however, when he warned that the church would be scattered on account of persecution and that most of the church would rebel against Christ, added something even more serious—there would be such confusion that Satan's chief follower would hold supreme power in the church and would preside there in place of God. Paul described that reign of abomination under the name of a single person because it is only one reign, although one succeeds another. We must understand that all the sects the church has been split up into have been like many streams of rebellion that started off by drawing water from the right course of water. However, the Muslims are an exception to this, as they were like a violent stream bursting its banks, taking half of the church in its wake. Antichrist also managed to infect the rest of the church with his poison. So we see with our own eyes that Paul's memorable prediction has been fulfilled.

There is nothing forced in my exposition here. Believers in Paul's day imagined they would be translated to heaven after enduring troubles for a short time. Paul, however, predicted that after they'd had enemies from a foreign country molesting them for some time, they would have more evils to endure from enemies at home. These enemies from within are those who made a profession of belonging to Christ but soon proved to be treacherous, inasmuch as God's temple itself would be polluted by sacrilegious tyranny, so that Christ's greatest enemy would exercise dominion there. The term **is revealed** denotes the clear possession of tyranny, as if Paul had said that the day of Christ would not come until this tyrant had openly manifested himself and had, as it were, deliberately overturned the whole order of the church.

4. He opposes and exalts himself over everything that is called God or is worshiped. The two epithets **man of lawlessness** and **man doomed to destruction** (verse 3) are closely linked. The dreadful confusion they cause would greatly disturb weak minds. They also manage to stir up godly people so that they worry that they may be degenerate like the others around them. Paul, however, now drew a picture to reveal the characteristics of the Antichrist. It may be readily seen from these words what the true nature of Satan's kingdom is and what it is made up of. When Paul says the Antichrist **opposes** God, he is saying that he will claim for himself those things that belong to God, so that he is wrongly worshiped in God's temple. The Antichrist places his kingdom in direct opposition to Christ's kingdom. So, because Christ's kingdom is a spiritual kingdom, this tyrant will wage war on souls, so that it may rival the kingdom of Christ. Later we will find that Paul assigned to him the power to deceive by employing wicked teaching and fake miracles. So if you want to know about the Antichrist, you must view him as being diametrically opposed to Christ.

Everything that is called God is translated by others as "everyone who is called." It may, however, be conjectured, both from the old translation and from some Greek commentaries, that Paul's words have been corrupted. It would have been easy to make a mistake with just one letter. For where was written *pan to* ("everything"), some transcriber or too daring a reader turned it into *panta* ("everyone"). This difference, however, is not so important, for Paul undoubtedly meant that Antichrist would grab for himself those things that belonged to God alone, so that he would **set himself up [above]** every divine claim, so that all religion and all worship of God might lie under his feet. This expression then, "everything that is reckoned to be God," is equivalent to "everything that is reckoned as divine," and *sebasma* (**is worshiped**) refers to the veneration God alone deserves.

Here, however, the subject under discussion is not the name of God but his majesty and worship and, in general, everything he claims for himself. "True religion consists of worshiping the true God alone. This is what the man of lawlessness has accrued to himself." Everyone who has learned from Scripture what things especially belong to God will have no great difficulty in recognizing the Antichrist as he observes the claims of the Pope, even if he is only a ten-year-old boy. Scripture declares that God alone is the Lawgiver. "There is only one Lawgiver and Judge, the one who is able to save and destroy" (James 4:12). Only God governs souls by his Word. He alone establishes divine worship and the rites linked with it. Scripture teaches that righteousness and salvation are to be found in Christ alone. It assigns, at the same time, how this is to be done.

There is not one of these things that the Pope does not claim to be under his authority. He boasts that it is in his power to bind consciences with such laws as seem good to him and subjects them to everlasting punishment. As far as the sacraments are concerned, he either institutes new ones, according to his own pleasure and fancy, or he corrupts and deforms those that have been instituted by Christ. He even ignores Christ's sacraments and replaces them with those of his own invention and commits abominable sacrileges as he does this. He contrives means of attaining salvation that are completely at variance with the teaching of the Gospel; in short, he does not hesitate to change the whole of religion for his own pleasure. When he robs God of his honor in this way, the Pope leaves God with an empty title of deity, while he transfers all divine power to himself. This is what Paul talks about a little later on: **proclaiming himself to be God**. As has been said, he does not insist upon the simple term *God* but intimates that the pride and arrogance of Antichrist would be such that, raising himself above everyone else, he climbs on to God's judgment seat. There he claims to rule not as a man but as God himself and with divine authority. We know that whatever takes the place of God is an idol, even when it appears to bear God's name.

In God's temple. This single phrase is sufficient to refute the error and foolishness of those who reckon the Pope to be Vicar of Christ on the grounds that he has his seat in the church. Paul places Antichrist nowhere else but in the very sanctuary of God. This is not a friend but an enemy close at hand, who opposes Christ under the very name of Christ. But, it is asked, why is the church pictured as the center of so many superstitions when it was destined to be the pillar of truth (see 1 Timothy 3:15)? In answer, it is represented in this way not on the ground that it retains all the qualities of the church, but because it does still possess *some* qualities of the church. Today it is **God's temple** in which the Pope rules, but at the same time he has profaned it with innumerable sacrileges.

Verses 5-8

Don't you remember that when I was with you I used to tell you these things? And now you know what is holding him back, so that he may be revealed at the proper time. For the secret power of lawlessness is already at work; but the one who now holds it back will continue to do so till he is taken out of the way. And then the lawless one will be revealed, whom the Lord Jesus will overthrow with the breath of his mouth and destroy by the splendor of his coming.

5. Don't you remember? This added no small weight to the teaching they had previously heard from Paul, so that they would not think he had made it up on the spur of the moment. Just as he had given them an early warning about the rule of Antichrist and the devastation that was coming on the church when such questions had not yet been asked about this, the apostle saw beyond all doubt that this teaching was especially important for the Thessalonians. And, unquestionably, that really was the case. The people Paul was writing to were destined to see many things that would trouble them. And when their posterity would see a large proportion of those who had made a profession of faith in Christ rebel against godliness, maddened as it were by a gadfly, or rather would plunge themselves into ruin like possessed people, what could they do but shake with fear? However, they would be given an invincible fortress for their protection. Events were so ordered by God, because of people's execrable and base ingratitude, that Antichrist and his followers would be judged by God. We may observe here how forgetful people are about matters that affect their everlasting salvation. We must also note Paul's forbearance. While he might have been greatly upset at the Thessalonians, he only rebuked them in a mild way. He reproved them in a fatherly way though they had forgotten such crucial things.

6. And now you know what is holding him back. *To katexon* (**holding . . . back**) means here an impediment or reason for delay. Chrysostom, who thinks this can only be understood to refer to the Spirit or to the Roman Empire, inclines to the latter opinion. He gives a plausible reason—because Paul would not have spoken about the Spirit in hidden or obscure terms, but in speaking about the Roman Empire he wanted to avoid arousing unnecessary aggravation. Chrysostom also states why the existence of the Roman Empire delayed the revelation of Antichrist. The kingdom of Babylon was overthrown by the Persians and Medes, and the Macedonians, after they had conquered the Persians, then captured the kingdom. The Romans then defeated the Macedonians. So Antichrist took hold of the vacant throne of the Roman Empire. All these events took place. Chrysostom is right as far as history is concerned. However, I think Paul had a different idea in mind—the thought that the teaching of the Gospel needed to be spread far and wide until nearly the whole world was guilty of deliberate malice toward God. The Thessalonians unquestionably had heard from Paul in person about this, for he told them to recall what he had previously taught them when he was with them.

So, my readers, you have to decide between these two interpretations. In the first interpretation, the power of the Roman Empire stood in the way of the rise of Antichrist, inasmuch as he could only ascend to the throne when it was vacant. In the second interpretation, Paul declared that the light of the Gospel must spread throughout the world before God gave Satan full rein. I think I can hear Paul teaching about the universal call of the Gentiles—that the grace of God must be offered to everyone—that Christ must enlighten the whole world with his Gospel, so that the godlessness of men might be fully demonstrated. Therefore, there was a delay until the work of the Gospel had been completed, a gracious invitation to accept the Gospel first of all being offered. Hence Paul added, **at the proper time**; the right time for vengeance was after grace had been rejected.

7. The secret power of lawlessness. This is contrasted with **that he may be revealed** (verse 6). As Satan had not yet become very strong, as he would be when Antichrist could openly oppress the church, Paul said that Satan is carrying on a secret and clandestine war until he makes his attacks publicly. Therefore Satan was secretly laying the foundations on which he would later stand, which is just what happened. This confirms that it is not one individual who is represented by Antichrist, but one kingdom that extends through many ages. John also says that Antichrist will come, but that there were already many in his time:

> *Dear children, this is the last hour; and as you have heard that the antichrist is coming, even now many antichrists have come. This is how we know it is the last hour. They went out from us, but they did not really belong to us. For if they had belonged to us, they would have remained with us; but their going showed that none of them belonged to us. But you have an anointing from the Holy One, and all of you know the truth. I do not write to you because you do not know the truth, but because you do know it and because no lie comes from the truth. Who is the liar? It is the man who denies that Jesus is the Christ. Such a man is the antichrist—he denies the Father and the Son. No one who denies the Son has the Father; whoever acknowledges the Son has the Father also.*
> —1 John 2:18-23

John was admonishing those who were then alive to be on their guard against this deadly disease, which at that time was springing up everywhere. Sects were rising up that were the seeds, as it were, of a deadly weed that nearly choked the good wheat God had sown in his field. Paul conveyed the secret nature of this evil work, but he used the word *mystery* when he alluded to salvation: "the mystery that has been kept hidden for ages and generations, but is now disclosed to the saints" (Colossians 1:26). Paul insisted that the crucial struggle is between the Son of God and this **man doomed to destruction** (verse 3), the son of perdition.

But the one who now holds it back. While the apostle made both statements about one person—that he will hold supremacy for a time and that he will shortly be eclipsed—I have no doubt that he refers both times to Antichrist. We must explain **holds ... back** in the future tense—"he will hold back." Paul, in my opinion, added this to comfort the believers. The reign of Antichrist will be temporary, for limits have been imposed on him by God. Because believers might object, "What is the purpose of preaching the Gospel if Satan is now hatching a tyranny that he will exert forever?" Paul advises them to be patient. God will allow the affliction of his church for a limited period only, so that one day he will rescue it. On the other hand, the everlasting nature of Christ's reign must be borne in mind, so that believers can draw comfort from it.

8. And then the lawless one will be revealed. That is, when the aforementioned impediment has been **taken out of the way** (verse 7). Paul did not say when this revelation will take place, but he did say that it will take place when he who now holds sway is taken out of the way, for the apostle had said there was some obstruction in the way of Antichrist's taking possession of the kingdom. Later he added that Antichrist was already hatching a secret evil work. The apostle interspersed comfort on the ground that this tyranny must at some time have an end. He now repeated that this **lawless one**, who had stayed hidden, would **be revealed**. He repeated this so believers, being equipped with spiritual armor, would nevertheless fight vigorously under Christ's banner and not allow themselves to be overwhelmed, though the deluge of impiety surrounds them.

Whom the Lord Jesus will overthrow. The apostle had foretold the destruction of Antichrist's reign, and now he says how this will take place. Antichrist will be reduced to nothing by the word of the Lord, by **the breath of his mouth**. It is not clear, however, whether he was speaking about Christ's last appearing, when he will be manifested from heaven as the Judge. The words indeed seem to have this meaning, but Paul did not mean that Christ would accomplish all this in one moment. Hence we must understand it in this sense: Antichrist will be wholly and in every respect destroyed and defeated when that final day of the restoration of all things arrives. Paul, however, intimates that Christ will in the meantime, by the rays of light he will emit before his coming, banish the darkness in which Antichrist will reign, just as the sun, before it is seen by us, chases away the darkness of the night by diffusing its rays everywhere.

Therefore, the victory of the Word will be seen in this world, for the

breath of his mouth refers to the Word, as it does in Isaiah 11:4, to which Paul appears to allude: "He will strike the earth with the rod of his mouth; with the breath of his lips he will slay the wicked." The prophet Isaiah uses the words "the rod of his mouth" and "the breath of his lips" as armaments of Christ to defeat his enemies. This is a most unusual commendation for true and sound teaching. It is sufficient to kill off all ungodliness, and it will always be victorious in its opposition to all the schemes of Satan. Also, a short time after it has been proclaimed, Christ will come.

When Paul added **the splendor of his coming,** he was intimating that the light of Christ's presence will swallow up the darkness of Antichrist. In the meantime, he indirectly intimates, Antichrist will be allowed to reign for a time, when Christ has in a manner withdrawn, as usually happens whenever he presents himself to us but we turn our back on him. Unquestionably, it is a sad and lamentable departure of Christ when he takes away from men his light, which they have rejected or received irreverently. Paul taught that by his presence alone all God's elect will be totally safe from all the schemes of Satan.

Verses 9-12

The coming of the lawless one will be in accordance with the work of Satan displayed in all kinds of counterfeit miracles, signs and wonders, and in every sort of evil that deceives those who are perishing. They perish because they refused to love the truth and so be saved. For this reason God sends them a powerful delusion so that they will believe the lie and so that all will be condemned who have not believed the truth but have delighted in wickedness.

9. The apostle confirms what he has said with a contrasting argument. As Antichrist cannot stand unless he acts like Satan, so he has to disappear as soon as Christ arrives. In short, as it is only in darkness that he reigns, the dawn of the day makes the thick darkness of his reign disappear. We now see Paul's plan. He meant to say that Christ would have no difficulty in destroying the tyranny of Antichrist, which was supported by no resources except those of Satan. In the meantime, he pointed out the distinguishing marks of **the lawless one—the work of Satan displayed in all kinds of counterfeit miracles, signs and wonders.** Without doubt, in order that this may be opposed to Christ's kingdom, this must consist partly of false teaching and partly of fake miracles. Christ's kingdom is made up of the doctrine of truth and the power of the Spirit. Satan, accordingly, with his aim of opposing Christ in the persons of his ministers, puts on Christ's mask and disguises himself with it. At the same time Antichrist also chooses armor so that he can, he thinks, defeat Christ with it. Christ, through the teaching of his Gospel, enlightens our minds and gives us eternal life. Antichrist, controlled by Satan through wicked doctrine, leads the wicked into eternal ruin and perdition. Christ puts forward the power of his Spirit for salvation and seals his Gospel with miracles. The adversary, Antichrist, through the work of Satan, alienates us from the Holy Spirit and by his delusions blinds men with his errors.

The apostle called Antichrist's miracles **all kinds of counterfeit miracles**. These include fake miracles that are contrived by cunning men with a view to delude the simple. **Counterfeit miracles** also embraces Satan's attacks on the genuine deeds of God, speaking against miracles in order to obscure God's glory. There can be no doubt that he also deceives through sorcery, as was seen in Pharaoh's magicians: "Pharaoh then summoned the wise men and sorcerers, and the Egyptian magicians also did the same things by their secret arts" (Exodus 7:11).

10. Those who are perishing. The apostle sees Satan's power as limited, for he is unable to harm God's elect, just as Christ also exempted them from this danger (see Matthew 24:24). From this it is apparent that Antichrist's power is controlled by what God allows him to do. This consolation was needed by the Thessalonians. All godly people would be overpowered by fear if it were not for this. So while Paul wanted them to be alert and on their guard in case they fell because of being careless, he also desired them to be hopeful because Satan's power is curbed. Satan is unable to defeat anyone, except for the wicked.

They perish because they refused to love the truth and so be saved. In case the wicked complain that they perish for no reason and claim to be innocent, saying they have been appointed to die because God is cruel rather than because of any fault on their side, Paul shows on what good grounds such severe vengeance from God will fall on them. They have not received in their minds the truths they have been presented with, and on their own accord they have refused God's salvation. This emphasizes more clearly what I have already said. The Gospel must be preached to the world before God lets Satan loose. God would never have allowed his temple to be so basely profaned had he not been provoked by the extreme ingratitude of men. In short, Paul declared that Antichrist will unwittingly be the minister of God's righteous vengeance against those who, being called to salvation, have rejected the Gospel and have preferred to apply their mind to ungodliness and error. Although the domination of Antichrist has been cruel, no people have perished except for those who deserved it, those who chose to. "But whoever fails to find me harms himself; all who hate me love death" (Proverbs 8:36). Unquestionably, though the voice of the Son of God is heralded everywhere, it falls on deaf ears belonging to hardened and obstinate people. While many people profess to be Christians, there are in reality few who have truly and wholeheartedly given themselves to Christ. So it is hardly surprising if a similar vengeance quickly follows such deplorable contempt.

The apostle uses the expression **they refused to love the truth** to mean that these people would not use their minds to love the Gospel. From this we learn that faith is always linked with a delightful and voluntary reverence for God; we do not correctly believe the Word of God unless it is viewed as a lovely and pleasant thing by us.

11. For this reason God sent them a powerful delusion. The apostle means that errors will not merely have a place, but the wicked will be blinded, so that they will rush headlong into ruin without thought. As God enlightens us inwardly by his Spirit, so that his teaching may be effective in us and so the eyes of our understanding may be opened, through a righteous judgment he gives those who reject him "over to a depraved mind" (Romans 1:28). God has appointed these people for destruction. They have closed eyes and senseless minds and act as if they have been bewitched as they hand themselves over to Satan and his followers to be deceived. Without doubt we have a clear example of this in the Papacy. No words can express what a monstrous and horrible nest of errors is there. How dreadfully superstitious and deluded the Papacy is! Nobody who has even a basic understanding of sound doctrine can think about such dreadful things without being overcome with horror. How, then, could the whole world hold them in high esteem unless men had been struck blind by the Lord and made, as it were, into mindless fools?

12. And so that all will be condemned who have not believed the truth. This means that such people will receive the punishment their godlessness deserves. So those who perish have no grounds for arguing with God, inasmuch as they reap their just deserts. We must keep in mind what is said in Deuteronomy 13:3: "The LORD your God is testing you to find out whether you love him with all your heart and with all your soul." The hearts of men are on trial. So let those who **have delighted in wickedness** reap the fruit of their actions. When Paul said, *all* **will be condemned,** he meant that contempt for God will not be hidden among the large number of people who refuse to obey the Gospel, for God judges the whole world. He is able to inflict his punishment on 100,000 people just as easily as he can judge one individual.

Have delighted in means, as it were, a voluntary inclination to evil. So the grateful are without excuse when they take so much delight **in wickedness,** which they choose instead of God's righteousness. Whom can they blame when they have deliberately rebelled against God and have ignored the guidance that would have led them to him? It is clear that they willingly and intentionally listened to false teachings.

Verses 13-14

But we ought always to thank God for you, brothers loved by the Lord, because from the beginning God chose you to be saved through the sanctifying work of the Spirit and through belief in the truth. He called you to this through our gospel, that you might share in the glory of our Lord Jesus Christ.

13. But we ought always to thank God for you. The apostle now made a clear distinction between the Thessalonians and the reprobates, so that their faith would not waver because of the rebellion that would take place. Paul was bearing in mind believers who would come later as well as the welfare of the Thessalonians. Paul did more than just emphasize that they would not fall over the same precipice the world would. Paul extolled the grace of God they had received so that they might continue to live in a secure and peaceful way that leads to life. Paul wanted them to be able to do this even though nearly all the rest of the world was rushing headlong into destruction, as if they were being carried along by a hurricane. We must think about the judgments of God on the reprobate in such a way that they are, as it were, mirrors that show us his mercy toward us. We must conclude that it is solely due to the special grace of God that we do not perish along with them.

The apostle called the Thessalonians **loved by the Lord** so that they would reflect on the fact that they had escaped from the almost universal destruction of the world only because of God's unmerited love toward them. Thus Moses admonished the Jews: "The LORD did not set his affection on you and choose you because you were more numerous than other peoples, for you were the fewest of all peoples. But it was because the LORD loved you and kept the oath he swore to your forefathers that he brought you out with a mighty hand and redeemed you from the land of slavery, from the power of Pharaoh king of Egypt" (Deuteronomy 7:7-8). When we hear the word *love*, we must at once remember John's statement about this: "We love because he [God] first loved us" (1 John 4:19). In short, Paul did two things here: he confirmed faith, so that the godly might not be overcome with fear, and he urged them to be grateful, so that they might value even more God's mercy toward them.

Because from the beginning God chose you. The apostle now explains why everyone is not involved and swallowed up in the same ruin—Satan has no power over anyone who has been chosen by God. Satan cannot stop them from being saved, even if heaven and earth should disappear. This verse can be read in a variety of ways. The old translation rendered it "first fruits" (*aparchen*). But as almost all Greek manuscripts have *ap' arches* ("from the beginning"), I prefer to follow that reading. If you prefer "first fruits," this would mean that believers have been, as it were, set aside for a sacred offering, in line with a metaphor from the ancient custom of the law. However, I think we should keep to the generally agreed translation of this verse, which says that the Thessalonians were chosen from the beginning. Some people think this means they were among the first to be called. But this is not what Paul means, and that does not fit into the context of the verses. Paul did not just exempt from fear a few individuals who had been led to Christ as soon as the Gospel was preached; this consolation applies to all God's elect, without exception.

When therefore the apostle said **from the beginning**, he meant there was no danger concerning their salvation, which is founded on God's eternal election. It cannot be defeated, no matter what tumultuous changes take place. "No matter how much Satan may confuse and confound everything in the world, your salvation has been put on a sound footing, before the creation of the world." Here, therefore, is the true port of safety—God, who **chose** us **from the beginning**, will rescue us from all evils that threaten us, for we have elected to receive salvation. We will, therefore, be safe from destruction. It is not our place to penetrate into God's secret counsel as we seek assurance about our salvation. However, God has given signs or tokens of our calling, which should be enough to gain the assurance we desire.

Through the sanctifying work of the Spirit and through belief in the truth. This may be explained in two ways: *with* sanctification or *by* sanctification. It hardly matters which of these two you choose, as Paul meant simply, having spoken about the election of God, to add these tokens of salvation that reveal his calling. To know we are called by God, there is no need to find out what God decreed before the creation of the world, for we find in ourselves all the evidence we need, if he has sanctified us by his Spirit and enlightened us in the faith of his Gospel. The Gospel is proof that we have been adopted by God, and the Spirit seals us. Those who are led by the Spirit are children of God (see Romans 8:14), and everyone who possesses Christ by faith has everlasting life (see 1 John 5:12). These things must be carefully noted so that we do not overlook the revelation of God's will in which he tells us to rest.

We would be immersed in a deep labyrinth if we tried to plummet the profound secret counsels of God; so Paul leads us away from any such investigation. We should rest satisfied with the faith of the Gospel and in the grace of the Spirit through which we have been brought to life. In this way the horrible wickedness of those who make God's election a basis for every kind of iniquity will be refuted. Paul links our calling with faith and regeneration in such a way that he does not allow us to view it on any other basis.

14. He called you to this through our gospel. The apostle next repeated the same thing but in rather different terms. For the sons of God are not called in any other way than to belief of the truth. Paul, however, meant to show here how competent a witness he was to confirm what he also ministered. He accordingly put himself forward as an example, that the Thessalonians might not doubt the Gospel in which they had been instructed by him. The Gospel is God's voice, which woke them up from death and delivered them from the tyranny of Satan. Paul called it **our** gospel not because it originated with him but because its preaching had been committed to him.

That you might share in the glory of our Lord Jesus Christ can be taken in an active or a passive way. It either means that the Thessalonians were called so that they might one day **share in** a **glory** with Christ or that Christ acquired them with a view to his **glory**. This was a second way to assure the Thessalonians about their faith in Christ. This truth would come to their defense, for they were nothing less than God's own inheritance. That would help them to strengthen their salvation and to defend God's glory.

Verses 15-17

So then, brothers, stand firm and hold to the teachings we passed on to you, whether by word of mouth or by letter. May our Lord Jesus Christ himself and God our Father, who loved us and by his grace gave us eternal encouragement and good hope, encourage your hearts and strengthen you in every good deed and word.

Paul based this exhortation on what he had previously written, for our perseverance and steadfastness rest on nothing other than the assurance of divine grace. When, however, God calls us to salvation, stretching out, as it were, his hand to us; when Christ, through the teaching of the Gospel, presents himself to us for our benefit; when the Spirit is given us as a seal and a guarantee of eternal life, even if the heavens should cave in, we must not become disheartened. Paul, accordingly, wanted the Thessalonians to stand not just when other people stand, but to be more settled and stable than them. Even if the Thessalonians saw nearly the whole world turning away from the faith, even if they saw that the world was in total confusion, they were to keep their footing. God's calling should strengthen us against all such pressures, so that even if the rest of the world is shaken, we will remain steady and firm.

15. So then, brothers, stand firm and hold to the teachings we passed on to you. Some commentators restrict this to precepts of external church government, but this does not satisfy me, for Paul was pointing out how we should **stand firm**. To be given this invincible strength is much greater than external discipline. In my opinion, Paul included all Christian teaching in these words. It is as if he said that they had a foundation on which they could stand, so long as they persevered in sound teaching, as they had been instructed by him. I do not deny that the word *paradoseis* (**teachings**) is rightly applied to the ordinances appointed by the churches in order to promote peace and to do everything in an orderly way. I also agree that it is used in this sense when human traditions are mentioned: "Thus you nullify the word of God for the sake of your tradition" (Matthew 15:6). Paul, however, used the term "tradition" in the next chapter (verse 6, NIV margin) to mean the rule he had laid down. The context, however, as I have said, requires that it be taken here to apply to all of the teaching in which they had been instructed. The matter under discussion was of supreme importance, so their faith would stay secure in the middle of a dreadful battle in the church.

Roman Catholic leaders are foolish to deduce from this that their traditions should be observed. They reason like this: "If it was right for Paul to command traditions to be followed, it is also right for other teachers to do the same. If it was a good and holy thing to observe the former, the latter should be observed as well." Even if you say this refers to the external government of the church, I believe these teachings or traditions were not thought up by Paul but came from God himself. For Paul declares elsewhere that it was never his intention to capture anyone's conscience, as neither he nor any other apostle was allowed to do this. "I am saying this for your own good, not to restrict you, but that you may live in a right way in undivided devotion to the Lord" (1 Corinthians 7:35). Roman Catholic leaders act in an even more high-handed way when they attempt to pass on their traditions as if they were Paul's traditions. We can say good-bye to these trifles when we understand Paul correctly. We can understand, to a certain extent, from this letter what traditions Paul did recommend, for he says, **whether by word of mouth or by letter**. What do these letters contain except pure doctrine that overturns the very foundation of the whole of the Papacy and every invention that differs from the simple Gospel?

16. May our Lord Jesus Christ himself. Paul ascribed to Christ a totally divine work and presented Christ, along with the Father, as the Author of the best divine blessings. This gives us a clear view of Christ's divinity, and in this way we are taught that we cannot receive anything from God unless we seek it in Christ himself. When Paul says that God will give us those things he has promised, he shows us clearly how little effect exhortations have unless God inwardly moves and changes our hearts. Unquestionably, these things will fall on deaf ears if Christian teaching is not brought to life by the Spirit.

What Paul added after this, **who loved us and by his grace gave us eternal encouragement and good hope**, refers to Paul's prayer for the Thessalonians. Paul wanted them to be certain that God would do for them what he now prayed for. How does Paul demonstrate this? By showing that they were dear to him. Paul had bound himself to them and conferred on them special favors. Paul now reminded them that they had **eternal encouragement**. The words **good hope** have the same purpose in mind—they could confidently expect a constant supply of divine gifts of grace.

17. What did Paul ask for? He prayed that God would sustain the hearts of the Thessalonians with divine comfort. It was part of God's work to keep the Thessalonians from giving in to anxiety; more than that, God would enable them to persevere, both in a godly and holy way of life and in sound doctrine.

2 Thessalonians
Chapter 3

Verses 1-5

Finally, brothers, pray for us that the message of the Lord may spread rapidly and be honored, just as it was with you. And pray that we may be delivered from wicked and evil men, for not everyone has faith. But the Lord is faithful, and he will strengthen and protect you from the evil one. We have confidence in the Lord that you are doing and will continue to do the things we command. May the Lord direct your hearts into God's love and Christ's perseverance.

1. **Finally, brothers, pray for us**. Paul was greatly strengthened by the Lord and surpassed everyone else in his earnest prayers. Nevertheless, he did not despise the prayers of believers. So we must follow his example, eagerly desire divine help, and stir up our Christian brothers and sisters to pray for us, through which the Lord plans to help us.

When, however, Paul added, **that the message of the Lord may spread rapidly,** he was not thinking about himself but was concerned for the entire church. Why did he wish the Thessalonians to pray for him? So the teaching of the Gospel would **spread rapidly**. He did not want people to focus their attention on him but on God's glory and the general welfare of the church. **Spread rapidly** means here dissemination. **Honored** means something else. Paul was asking that his preaching might have in it power and effectiveness to renew men in the image of God. Hence, when Christians lead a holy and upright life, they are honoring the Gospel. On the other hand, people bring the Gospel into disrepute when they profess to be Christians with their mouths but live wicked lives. Paul says, **just as it was with you.** This should stimulate the godly to want everyone else to be like them in honoring the Gospel. So those who have already entered the kingdom of God are exhorted to pray daily that it may come (see Matthew 6:10).

2. The **wicked and evil men** Paul referred to were treacherous people who lurked in the church, bearing the name of Christians, or at least Jews, but who with a mad zeal for the law persecuted all followers of the Gospel. Paul knew what great danger Christians faced from these groups of people. Chrysostom thought that only people who oppose the Gospel with false and perverse teaching are meant here. He excuses people who used violence such as Alexander, Hymenaeus, and others. But I think this can be extended to include all kinds of dangers and enemies. At that time Paul himself was traveling toward Jerusalem, and he wrote this letter in the middle of his journey. Paul had been forewarned by God that he would face imprisonments and persecutions in Jerusalem (see Acts 20:22-23). When Paul said, **that we may be delivered,** he meant that he might be victorious, whether he died or had his life spared.

For not everyone has faith. This could mean, "Faith is not in everyone." This expression, however, is both ambiguous and obscure. We should remember that faith is a gift of God that is not found in everyone. Many pretend to come to him, but their hearts are far from him. Further, Paul does not speak about everyone indiscriminately but merely refers to those who belong to the church—the Thessalonians saw that many people did not have genuine faith. Indeed, they saw how few people were true believers. It would have been unnecessary to say this to strangers, but Paul simply said that not all who profess faith possess real faith. There is no question that Paul singled out those he came into contact with. It is probable there were those who, while they had the appearance of being godly, were nevertheless far from this in reality. From this came the conflict Paul was talking about.

Paul had good reason to ask the Thessalonians to pray that he should **be delivered from wicked and evil men.** Paul said that faith is not possessed by everyone, because the wicked and reprobate are always mixed with the good. "But while everyone was sleeping, his enemy came and sowed weeds among the wheat, and went away" (Matthew 13:25). Whenever we are under fire from wicked people who nevertheless ask to be recognized as belonging to the Christian circle, we should remember that **not everyone has faith.** Our faith is bound to buckle unless we remember that among those who profess to follow Christ and bear his name there are many unbelieving, disloyal, and treacherous people.

3. But the Lord is faithful. The Thessalonians might have been influenced by unfavorable reports about Paul and so entertained doubts about his ministry. But Paul had taught them that men are not always faithful, and now he called the Thessalonians back to God. Paul said, **the Lord is faithful** in order to strengthen them against all the devices of men, which are used to upset Christians. "Such men are indeed treacherous, but there is in God a support that is abundantly secure, which enables you to keep going." The apostle said the Lord is **faithful** in order to stick to his purpose of encouraging the Thessalonians not to give up, reminding them that God would never forsake them in danger. "God is faithful; he will not let you be tempted beyond what you can bear" (1 Corinthians 10:13).

These words show that Paul was more concerned about the welfare of the Thessalonians than about his own welfare. Malicious people opposed Paul, and the full weight of their attacks fell on him. But Paul was taken up with anxious thoughts about the Thessalonians, in case they were injured by their trials.

The term **evil** may refer to the malice of the evil people who were attacking the Thessalonians. However, I prefer to interpret it as referring to Satan, **the evil one**, the leader of all wicked people. It would be of little help to be rescued from the deceit and attacks of men if the Lord did not protect us from all spiritual attacks.

4. We have confidence in the Lord that you are doing and will continue to do . . . The apostle prepared the way for giving instructions with this introduction, for the **confidence** he said he had about the Thessalonians made them willing to obey Paul's commands. Paul said, however, that the hope that he had in them was founded on **the Lord**, inasmuch as he was the one able to give them obedient hearts. However, it is probable that this expression shows that it was not Paul's intention to instruct them in anything other than the Lord's commandments. Note then the limits that he prescribed both for himself and for them: for himself, not to command anything that did not come from the Lord; for them, not to give obedience to anyone except the Lord. Everyone who does not observe this limitation is not following Paul's example but is binding the church and subjecting it to man-made laws.

Paul might also have had in mind that he needed to ensure that the Thessalonians respected his apostleship, especially in the face of wicked people who were trying to dishonor it. Paul's next prayer appears to support this argument. As long as men's hearts continue to be directed toward **God's love and Christ's perseverance** (verse 5), other things will work out. Paul declared that he wanted nothing but this. From this it is clear how far he was from seeking personal power. He was content so long as the Thessalonians persevered in the love of God and in the hope of Christ's coming. After Paul had declared his confidence in this matter, he commanded us to not relax our earnest prayers since we too are looking forward with hope.

Paul summarizes here what he knew Christians most needed to know. Everyone should aim to excel in these two things. Unquestionably, the love of God cannot reign in us unless we also exercise brotherly love. Waiting for Christ teaches us to disdain the world, to mortify the flesh, and to endure the cross. At the same time the expression **Christ's perse-**

verance might mean Christ's teaching being born in us. However, I prefer to understand it as referring to the hope of ultimate redemption. Waiting for the Redeemer is the only thing that sustains us in the warfare of the present life. This waiting requires endurance as we take up Christ's cross.

Verses 6-10

In the name of the Lord Jesus Christ, we command you, brothers, to keep away from every brother who is idle and does not live according to the teaching you received from us. For you yourselves know how you ought to follow our example. We were not idle when we were with you, nor did we eat anyone's food without paying for it. On the contrary, we worked night and day, laboring and toiling so that we would not be a burden to any of you. We did this, not because we do not have the right to such help, but in order to make ourselves a model for you to follow. For even when we were with you, we gave you this rule: "If a man will not work, he shall not eat."

The apostle now moved on to correcting a particular fault. Among the Thessalonians there were some lazy people who were also curious and who never stopped spreading gossip. They wandered from house to house, trying to scrape together a living at other people's expense. Paul forbade the Thessalonians from encouraging through their generosity the indolence of such people. Paul taught them that the correct way to earn money for the necessities of life is by engaging in useful work. Paul applied this principle not to those living a dissolute life or to known criminals, but to people who were too lazy to do an honest day's work.

Idleness causes disorder. If we ignore the reason we were made, we will leave chaos in our wake. It is only when we live by the rule that God has given that our lives are correctly regulated. Once this way of living is set aside, nothing but confusion remains. This should also be noted by anyone who is tempted to ignore God's commands. God has created us so we can be useful to other people. So the person who only lives for himself and who even becomes a burden to the rest of society is rightly called **idle**. He is not living **according to the teaching** he has received. Paul declares that such people should be ousted from the fellowship of believers so they do not bring shame on the church.

6. In the name of the Lord Jesus Christ, we command you. Erasmus translates this: "*by* the name," as if Paul were pleading with the Thessalonians. While I do not completely reject this, I think the particle **in** is redundant, as is the case in many other passages and in line with the Hebrew idiom. So the meaning is that this commandment should be welcomed with reverence, not as from a mere mortal man, but as from Christ himself. Chrysostom agrees with this explanation. This withdrawal, however (**keep away from**), about which Paul spoke does not refer to public excommunication but to private fellowship. He forbids believers to form strong relationships with these kind of drones, who have no honorable means of supporting themselves. Paul says **keep away from every brother** because if they profess to be Christians, they are like vermin that pollute the good name of Christianity.

Who . . . does not live according to the teaching you received from us. That is, the teaching that is about to follow: food should not be given to people who refuse to do a day's work. Before Paul mentioned this, he stated what example he himself had given them in this. Teaching becomes much more credible and authoritative when we do not ask others to do something we have not done. **We worked night and day, laboring and toiling so that we would not be a burden to any of you** (verse 8). Paul had also mentioned this in his previous letter to the Thessalonians.

As for Paul's saying, **nor do we eat anyone's food without paying for it** (verse 8), he could not have done this unless he had engaged in hard manual labor. Paul had inconsiderate people in mind here—those who did not think ministers deserved a fair wage for their work. Some people are so mean that although they themselves make no contribution toward the pay of ministers, they still complain about their being paid at all, as if they were lazy people. Paul immediately said that he waived his right, declining to receive any remuneration from the Thessalonians. When Paul wrote, **in order to make ourselves a model for you to follow** (verse 9), he did not mean his example should be seen by the Thessalonians as a law, but that they knew what to do because they had seen his example with their own eyes.

9. Not because we do not have the right to such help. Paul wanted the Thessalonians to follow the example he set them about work. He did not want them to be like drones that do not make any honey and yet live on the work of other bees. We note how kind and thoughtful Paul was in this matter. He did not insist on his rights and was completely different from those who abuse their positions of power as they pursue their own selfish ambitions. There was a danger that the Thessalonians might think that because he gave his services free of charge, this should be the pattern for all future ministers. This could happen through the mean disposition of people. Paul, anticipating this danger, taught that he did have the right to receive payment for his preaching, so that other preachers would not be expected to preach for nothing in the future. Paul wanted to expose those who are so ready to grumble about money being paid to ministers, even though they themselves make no financial contribution to that cause.

10. "If a man will not work, he shall not eat." "You will eat the fruit of your labor" (Psalm 128:2). "Lazy hands make a man poor, but diligent hands bring wealth" (Proverbs 10:4). It is certain that God disapproves of indolence and idleness. In addition to this, we know that man was created to do something. Scripture teaches us this, and nature itself teaches the same lesson to the ungodly. So it is only reasonable that those who wish to be exempt from the common law should also be deprived of food, the reward of labor. When, however, the apostle commanded that such people should not eat, he did not mean that he ordered that such people should not eat; rather, he forbade the Thessalonians from encouraging their laziness by providing them with food.

It should also be noted that there are a variety of ways of working. Whoever helps society in general, through his work, through bringing up a family, through the administration of public or private affairs, by counseling, or teaching, or working in any other way, is not to be numbered with the idle. Paul censures those lazy drones who lived off other people's labor, while they contributed nothing to help the human race. Some of our monks and priests who live pampered lives are guilty of this.

Verses 11-13

We hear that some among you are idle. They are not busy; they are busybodies. Such people we command and urge in the Lord Jesus Christ to settle down and earn the bread they eat. And as for you, brothers, never tire of doing what is right.

11. We hear that some among you are idle. It is probable that these kinds of drones were, so to speak, the seeds for idle monks. For from the beginning there were some people who, under the pretext of religion, either ate at other people's tables without paying for their food or deceived simple people into providing for them. They had become so numerous in Augustine's day that he decided to write a book denouncing idle monks. In it Augustine attacks their pride because they reject these admonitions from Paul's letters. They do not excuse themselves from work on the grounds of ill health but because they think they will be seen to be holier than other people if they never work. Augustine points out that while senators and nobles turn their hands to work, mechanics and laborers remain idle. The latter pretend to be engaged in holy living. Their only religion is to be well-fed and to be free from all work. This way of life they dignify with the name of their Order or with a particular Rule of this or that saint.

But what does the Spirit say through Paul's words? He labels them as **busybodies**. It is unnecessary here to go into detail about the idle life led by monks. There is a memorable saying of an old monk, recorded by Socrates in his *Tripartite History*, book viii, that he who does not work with his hands is like a plunderer. I could mention other examples, but they are unnecessary. Paul says such people are dissolute and in a way lawless. That is sufficient for us.

They are not busy; they are busybodies. In the Greek there is a play on words that is reflected in this translation—they were not *busy* but were *busy*bodies. Paul accused idle people of being guilty of unnecessary rushing around as they made a nuisance of themselves to other people. We observe that those who have nothing to do are more worn out doing nothing than they would be if they lived active lives. Wherever they go, they appear to be tired. They collect all kinds of information and then spread gossip in all their conversations. You would think they bore the weight of governing a country on their shoulders. Because this condition has such a negative effect on society, Paul told the Thessalonians they should not encourage idleness in anyone.

12. Such people we command and urge in the Lord Jesus Christ. Paul now corrects both faults he has mentioned—an irritating restlessness and doing no work. In the first place, they are to **settle down** and live a quiet life. That is, to live quietly within the limits of their calling, or as we often say, *"sans faire bruit"* (without making a noise). The most peaceful of all people are those who engage in lawful employment. People who have nothing to do make trouble for themselves as well as for others. In addition to this Paul adds another admonition—they should **earn the bread they eat.** Paul means here that they should be content with what belongs to them and should not be unreasonable toward other people. "Drink water," says Solomon, "from your own cistern, running water from your own well" (Proverbs 5:15).

It is only reasonable that every person should make use of what belongs to him or her. People should not swallow up, like a bottomless abyss, everything that belongs to others but should show generosity toward their neighbors, so their abundance can relieve a neighbor's need. In the same way, the apostle exhorted those who had been idle to work, not just so they would gain a livelihood for themselves, but so they could provide for the necessities of their brethren. Paul teaches this elsewhere as well: "He who has been stealing must steal no longer, but must work, doing something useful with his own hands, that he may have something to share with those in need" (Ephesians 4:28).

13. And as for you, brothers, never tire of doing what is right. Ambrose thinks this is added in case the rich should, because of a mean spirit, refuse to help the poor, since Paul had exhorted them to **earn the bread they eat** (verse 12). Unquestionably, we see that many people will use any ingenious excuse to act in an inhumane way. Chrysostom explains it like this: Idle people, no matter how right it is to condemn them, must nevertheless be helped when they are in need. I think Paul was trying to guard against giving unnecessary offense that might stem from the few people who were idle. It is usually the case that those who are often generous withdraw their help when they see their aid is not beneficial. Here we have a statement that is worthy of particular note—no matter how ungrateful, morose, proud, arrogant some poor people may be, no matter how much they annoy and irritate us, we must nevertheless never stop trying to be of assistance to them.

Verses 14-18

If anyone does not obey our instruction in this letter, take special note of him. Do not associate with him, in order that he may feel ashamed. Yet do not regard him as an enemy, but warn him as a brother. Now may the Lord of peace himself give you peace at all times and in every way. The Lord be with all of you. I, Paul, write this greeting in my own hand, which is the distinguishing mark in all my letters. This is how I write. The grace of our Lord Jesus Christ be with you all.

14. If anyone does not obey our instruction in this letter. Paul had previously said that he gave no commands that did not come from the Lord. So people who disobeyed what Paul said were not just rebelling against man but against God himself. Paul taught that such people should be severely disciplined. First, Paul asked that they be reported to him so he could deal with them with the authority that had been given to him. Second, Paul ordered them to be excommunicated so that as they were brought low by shame, they would repent. From this we infer that we must not spare the reputation of those who will not change unless they are exposed. We must take great care in explaining to the doctor the exact nature of others' disease so that he can prescribe the correct medicine for their cure.

Do not associate with him. I am sure this means to excommunicate him. Previously Paul had written, **keep away from every brother who is idle** (verse 6) since they lived in such a disorderly way. And now Paul says, **Do not associate with him,** for such a person had rejected his admonition. Paul was saying something in this second exhortation that was not present in the first. It is one thing to withdraw from intimate acquaintance with an individual, but quite another to keep totally aloof from his presence. In short, those who are disobedient after they have been disciplined Paul excluded from the fellowship of believers. From this we conclude that we should use the discipline of excommunication against hardened and obstinate people who will not otherwise allow themselves to turn from evil. Such people have to be branded with disgrace until, having been brought low and subdued, they learn to obey.

In order that he may feel ashamed. There are, it is true, other benefits that stem from excommunication—a disease can be stopped from infecting other people, so that one person's wickedness does not bring disgrace on the whole church. If one person is excommunicated, it serves as a severe warning to everyone else, who should then live in a spirit of awe and reverence toward God. "Those who sin are to be rebuked publicly, so that the others may take warning" (1 Timothy 5:20). Paul was dealing with just one of the benefits of excommunication: those who have sinned may be shamed into repentance. People who indulge their sins become more and more set in their evil ways. Therefore the best remedy is when a feeling of shame is aroused in the heart of the offender, so that he begins to be displeased with himself. It would be only a limited victory to shame individuals. Paul had something more in mind. He wanted the offender to make progress. He desired the guilty one to see his own evil ways and so be led into a purer way of living. Shame, like sorrow, is a useful preparation for hating sin. Everyone who deliberately persists in open sin, as I have said, must be bridled, in case their audacity should become greater as they see that no one curbs their evil activities.

15. Yet do not regard him as an enemy. Paul immediately added a softening touch to his admonition. As he commanded elsewhere, we must take care that the offender is not overwhelmed by sadness. "If anyone has caused grief, he has not so much grieved me as he has grieved all of you, to some extent—not to put it too severely. The punishment inflicted on him by the majority is sufficient for him. Now instead, you ought to forgive and comfort him, so that he will not be overwhelmed by excessive sorrow" (2 Corinthians 2:5-7). So we see that the aim of discipline is the benefit of the person on whom the church inflicts the punishment. If the punishment becomes out of hand, the wound will be too deep. So if we want to do good, gentleness and kindness are necessary so that those who are disciplined may know they are also loved. In short, excommunication does not lead to people being driven away from the Lord's flock but rather brings back those who have been wandering away.

We must observe, however, how Paul intended brotherly love to be shown—not through flattery or bribes but by admonitions. Then all but the totally incurable will feel that people are concerned for their welfare. In the meantime, excommunication should be differentiated from pronouncing a curse on someone. Paul told the members of the church who handed out admonitions to remember that the purpose was not that offenders should be cast out forever, as if they were cut off from all hope of salvation. Paul told them they must keep on trying to win back those who have strayed.

16. Now may the Lord of peace himself give you peace at all times and in every way. This prayer seems to be linked with the preceding sentence. Paul was encouraging the Thessalonians to seek peaceful solutions in everything they did. He had told them offenders should not be treated as rebellious and obstinate enemies. The aim was to bring offenders back with a sound mind through brotherly admonitions. So after these kinds of exhortations it was appropriate for Paul to tell them to cultivate peace. As this is a divine work, Paul prayed that it might occur. Nevertheless, Paul's prayer had the effect of being a precept. At the same time, he may also have had something else in mind—that God may restrain the disobedient and unruly so that they may not disturb the peace of the church.

17. I, Paul, write this greeting in my own hand, which is the distinguishing mark in all my letters. Paul was again taking steps to avoid a danger he had previously mentioned—**If anyone does not obey . . . this letter** (verse 14). He was guarding against forged letters that purported to be from him finding their way into the churches. This was an old trick of Satan—to send out spurious letters in order to detract from the genuine ones. These fake letters that bore the names of the apostles attempted to spread false teaching in a quest to corrupt the church. Through God's special kindness the fraudulent letters were exposed, and the teaching of Christ has come down to us sound and complete through the ministry of Paul and others.

18. The grace of our Lord Jesus Christ be with you all. The concluding prayer explains how God helps his believing people—by the presence of Christ's grace.